Edward Everett

The Questions of the Day

An Address, Delivered in the Academy of Music, in New York

Edward Everett

The Questions of the Day
An Address, Delivered in the Academy of Music, in New York

ISBN/EAN: 9783337087357

Printed in Europe, USA, Canada, Australia, Japan

Cover: Foto ©ninafisch / pixelio.de

More available books at **www.hansebooks.com**

The Questions of the Day.

AN ADDRESS,

DELIVERED IN THE ACADEMY OF MUSIC, IN NEW YORK,
ON THE FOURTH OF JULY, 1861.

BY

EDWARD EVERETT.

NEW YORK:
GEO. P. PUTNAM, 532 BROADWAY.
1861.

The Questions of the Day.

AN ADDRESS,

DELIVERED IN THE ACADEMY OF MUSIC, IN NEW YORK,
ON THE FOURTH OF JULY, 1861.

BY

EDWARD EVERETT.

NEW YORK:
GEO. P. PUTNAM, 532 BROADWAY.
1861.

CORRESPONDENCE.

New York, 28th *May*, 1861.

Hon. Edward Everett,

Dear Sir:—The undersigned, having read your late speech at Roxbury with deep satisfaction, and knowing that many of their fellow-citizens regard it as a true and eloquent expression of the feelings of the aroused patriotic, national heart, concerning the great events and exigencies of the day, and believing that a similar address by you in this city would be of great public utility, respectfully request you to address the citizens of New York, at the Academy of Music, at the earliest date that will suit your convenience.

Gardiner Spring,	L. Bradish,
M. H. Grinnell,	Horatio Potter,
John J. Cisco,	George Bancroft,
August Belmont,	Hamilton Fish,
Moses Taylor,	Valentine Mott,
Wilson G. Hunt,	Henry W. Bellows,
Thomas De Witt,	John A. Dix,
George Potts,	William H. Aspinwall,
Peter Cooper,	George Griswold, jun.,
J. R. Whiting,	Wm. Curtis Noyes,
James Harper,	Stephen H. Tyng,
Wm. E. Dodge,	Jas. T. Brady,
Daniel F. Tieman,	Saml. B. Betts,
S. Draper,	Wm. B. Taylor, P. M.,
Geo. P. Morris,	Royal Phelps,
Geo. W. Blunt,	Alex. W. Bradford,
Chas. Scribner,	N. P. Willis,
D. P. Ingraham,	Wm. H. Appleton,
Wm. M. Evarts,	Henry J. Raymond,
S. Irenæus Prime.	Horace Greeley.

Boston, 20th *June*, 1861.

Gentlemen:

I have received this day your letter of the 28th ult., inviting me to deliver an address, in the Academy of Music, on the great issues now before the country. I feel much honored by such a call, and I shall have great pleasure in obeying it at an early day. It has been suggested to me that the Fourth of July would, as a public holiday, be a convenient day for the purpose. The anniversary of the Great Declaration would certainly be an appropriate occasion for an attempt to vindicate the principles, now so formidably assailed, on which the Independence of the United States, as ONE PEOPLE, was originally asserted.

I am, Gentlemen, most respectfully yours,

EDWARD EVERETT.

P. S.—Understanding that it is proposed to issue tickets of admission, I would respectfully suggest that the proceeds should be applied to the relief of the families of the New York Volunteers.

To Hon. L. BRADISH, and the other Gentlemen, whose
    names are subscribed to the invitation.

ADDRESS.*

BY EDWARD EVERETT.

----•••----

WHEN the Congress of the United States, on the 4th of July, 1776, issued the ever memorable Declaration which we commemorate to-day, they deemed that a decent respect for the opinions of mankind required a formal statement of the causes which impelled them to the all-important measure. The eighty-fifth anniversary of the great Declaration finds the loyal people of the Union engaged in a tremendous conflict, to maintain and defend the grand nationality, which was asserted by our Fathers, and to prevent their fair Creation from crumbling into dishonorable Chaos. A great People, gallantly struggling to keep a noble framework of government from falling into wretched fragments, needs no justification at the tribunal of the public opinion of mankind. But while our patriotic fellow-citizens, who have rallied to the defence of the Union, marshalled by the ablest of living chieftains, are risking their lives in the field; while the blood of your youthful heroes and ours is poured out together in defence of this precious legacy of constitutional freedom, you will not think it a misappropriation of the hour, if I employ it in showing the justice of the cause in which we are engaged, and the fallacy of the arguments employed by the South, in vindication of the war, alike murderous and suicidal, which she is waging against the Constitution and the Union.

PROSPEROUS STATE OF THE COUNTRY LAST YEAR.

A twelvemonth ago, nay, six or seven months ago, our country was regarded and spoken of by the rest of the civilized world, as among the most prosperous in the family of nations. It was classed with England, France, and Russia, as one of the four leading powers of the age.† Remote as we were from the complications of foreign politics, the extent of our commerce and the efficiency of our navy won for us the respectful consideration of Europe. The United States were particularly referred to, on all occasions and in all countries, as an illustration of the mighty influence of free governments in promoting the prosperity of States. In England, notwithstanding some diplomatic collisions on boundary questions and occasional hostile reminiscences of the past, there has hardly been a debate for thirty years in parliament on any topic, in reference to which this country in the

---

* Delivered, by request, at the Academy of Music, New York, July 4, 1861. Large portions of this address were, on account of its length, necessarily omitted in the delivery.
† The Edinburgh Review for April, 1861, p. 555.

nature of things afforded matter of comparison, in which it was not referred to as furnishing instructive examples of prosperous enterprise and hopeful progress. At home, the country grew as by enchantment. Its vast geographical extent, augmented by magnificent accessions of conterminous territory peacefully made ; its population far more rapidly increasing than that of any other country, and swelled by an emigration from Europe such as the world has never before seen ; the mutually beneficial intercourse between its different sections and climates, each supplying what the other wants ; the rapidity with which the arts of civilization have been extended over a before unsettled wilderness, and, together with this material prosperity, the advance of the country in education, literature, science, and refinement, formed a spectacle, of which the history of mankind furnished no other example. That such was the state of the country six months ago was matter of general recognition and acknowledgment at home and abroad.

THE PRESIDENTIAL ELECTION AND ITS RESULTS

There was, however, one sad deduction to be made, not from the truth of this description, not from the fidelity of this picture for that is incontestable, but from the content, happiness, and mutual good will which ought to have existed on the part of a People, favored by such an accumulation of Providential blessings. I allude, of course, to the great sectional controversies which have so long agitated the country, and arrayed the people in bitter geographical antagonism of political organization and action. Fierce party contentions had always existed in the United States, as they ever have and unquestionably ever will exist under all free elective governments ; and these contentions had, from the first, tended somewhat to a sectional character. They had not, however, till quite lately, assumed that character so exclusively, that the minority in any one part of the country had not had a respectable electoral representation in every other. Till last November, there has never been a Southern Presidential Candidate, who did not receive electoral votes at the North, nor a Northern Candidate who did not receive electoral votes at the South.

At the late election and for the first time, this was not the case ; and consequences the most extraordinary and deplorable have resulted. The country, as we have seen, being in profound peace at home and abroad, and in a state of unexampled prosperity—Agriculture, Commerce, Navigation, Manufactures, East, West, North, and South recovered or rapidly recovering from the crisis of 1857—powerful and respected abroad, and thriving beyond example at home, entered in the usual manner upon the electioneering campaign, for the choice of the nineteenth President of the United States. I say in the usual manner, though it is true that parties were more than usually broken up and subdivided. The normal division was into two great parties, but there had on several former occasions been three ; in 1824 there were four, and there were four last November. The South equally with the West and the North entered into the canvass : conventions were held, nominations made, mass meetings assembled ; the platform, the press enlisted with unwonted vigor ; the election in all its stages, conducted in legal and constitutional form, without violence and without surprise, and the result obtained by a decided majority.

No sooner, however, was this result ascertained, than it appeared on the part of one of the Southern States, and her example was rapidly followed by others, that it had by no means been the intention of those States to abide by the result of the election, except on the one condition, of the choice of their candidate. The reference of the great sectional controversy to the peaceful arbitrament of the ballot box, the great safety valve of republican institutions, though made with every appearance of good faith, on the part of our brethren at the South, meant but this : if we succeed in this election, as we have in fifteen that have preceded it, well and good ; we will consent to govern the country for four years more, as we have already governed it for sixty years ; but we have no intention of acquiescing in any other result. We do not mean to abide by the election, although we participate in it, unless our candidate is chosen. If he fails we intend to prostrate the Government and break up the Union ; peaceably, if the States composing the majority are willing that it should be broken up peaceably ; otherwise, at the point of the sword.

SOUTH CAROLINA SECEDES FROM THE UNION.

The election took place on the 6th of November, and in pursuance of the extraordinary programme just described, the State of South Carolina, acting by a Convention chosen for the purpose, assembled on the 17th of December, and on the 20th, passed unanimously what was styled " an ordinance to dissolve the Union between the State of South Carolina and other States united with her, under the compact entitled the Constitution, of the United States of America." It is not my purpose on this occasion to make a documentary speech, but as this so-called " Ordinance " is very short, and affords matter for deep reflection, I beg leave to recite it in full :—

" We, the People of the State of South Carolina, in Convention assembled, do declare and ordain, and it is hereby declared and ordained, that the ordinance adopted by us in Convention on the 23d day of May, in the year of our Lord 1788, whereby the Constitution of the United States was ratified, and also all acts and parts of acts of the general assembly of this State, ratifying the amendments of the said Constitution, are hereby repealed, and that the Union now subsisting between South Carolina and other States, under the name of the United States of America, is dissolved."

This remarkable document is called an " Ordinance," and no doubt some special virtue is supposed to reside in the name. But names are nothing except as they truly represent things. An ordinance, if it is any thing clothed with binding force, is a Law, and nothing but a Law, and as such this ordinance, being in direct violation of the Constitution of the United States, is a mere nullity. The Constitution contains the following express provision : "This Constitution and the Laws of the United States made in pursuance thereof, and the treaties made or which shall be made under the authority of the United States, shall be the supreme law of the land, and the judges in every State shall be bound thereby, any thing in the Constitution or laws of any State to the contrary notwithstanding." Such being the express provision of the Constitution of the United States, which the people of South Carolina adopted in 1788, just as much as they ever adopted either of their State Constitutions, is it not trifling with serious things to claim that, by the simple expedient of passing a law under the name of an ordinance, this provision and every other provision of it may be nullified, and every magistrate and officer in Carolina, whether of the State or Union, absolved from the oath which they have taken to support it?

But this is not all. This secession ordinance purports to "repeal" the ordinance of 23d May, 1788, by which the Constitution of the United States was ratified by the people of South Carolina. It was intended, of course, by calling the act of ratification an ordinance to infer a right of repealing it by another ordinance. It is important, therefore, to observe that the act of ratification is not, and was not at the time called, an ordinance, and contains nothing which by possibility can be repealed. It is in the following terms:—

"The Convention [of the people of South Carolina], having maturely considered the Constitution, or form of government, reported to Congress by the convention of delegates from the United States of America, and submitted to them, by a resolution of the Legislature of this State passed the 17th and 18th days of February last, in order to form a more perfect Union, establish justice, ensure domestic tranquillity, provide for the common defence, promote the general welfare, and secure the blessings of liberty to the people of the said United States and their posterity, do, in the name and in behalf of the people of this State, hereby assent to and ratify the same."

Here it is evident that there is nothing in the instrument which, in the nature of things, can be repealed; it is an authorized solemn assertion of the People of South Carolina, that they assent to, and ratify a form of government, which is declared in terms to be paramount to all State laws and constitutions. This is a great historical fact, the most important that can ever occur in the history of a people. The fact that the People of South Carolina, on the 23d of May, 1788, assented to and ratified the Constitution of the United States, in order, among other objects, to secure the blessings of liberty for themselves and " their posterity," can no more be repealed in 1861, than any other historical fact that occurred in Charleston in that year and on that day. It would be just as rational, at the present day, to attempt by ordinance to repeal any other event, as that the sun rose or that the tide ebbed and flowed on that day, as to repeal by ordinance the assent of Carolina to the Constitution.

Again : it is well known that various amendments to the Constitution were desired and proposed in different States. The first of the amendments proposed by South Carolina was as follows :—

"Whereas it is essential to the preservation of the rights reserved to the several States and the freedom of the People under the operation of the General Government, that the right of prescribing the manner, times, and places of holding the elections of the Federal Legislature should be *forever inseparably* annexed to the sovereignty of the States ; this Convention doth declare that the same ought to remain to *all posterity*, a perpetual and fundamental right in the *local*, exclusive of the interference of the *general* Government, except in cases where the Legislature of the States shall refuse or neglect to perform or fulfil the same, according to the tenor of the said Constitution."

Here you perceive that South Carolina herself in 1788 desired a provision to be made and annexed inseparably to her sovereignty, that she should forever have the power of prescribing the time, place, and manner of holding the elections of members of Congress ;—but even in making this express reservation, to operate for all posterity, she was willing to provide that, if the State Legislatures refuse or neglect to perform the duty, (which is precisely the case of the Seceding States at the present day,) then the General Government was, by this South Carolina amendment, expressly authorized to do it. South Carolina in 1788, by a sort of prophetic foresight, looked forward to the possibility that the States might " refuse or neglect " to coöperate in carrying on the Government, and admitted, in that case, that the General Government must go on, in spite of their delinquency.

I have dwelt on these points at some length, to show how futile is the attempt, by giving the name of " ordinance " to the act, by which South Carolina adopted the Constitution, and entered the Union, to gain a power to leave it by a subsequent ordinance of repeal.*

IS SECESSION A CONSTITUTIONAL RIGHT, OR IS IT REVOLUTION?

Whether the present unnatural civil war is waged by the South, in virtue of a supposed constitutional right to leave the Union at pleasure ; or whether it is an exercise of the great and ultimate right of revolution, the existence of which no one denies, seems to be left in uncertainty by the leaders of the movement. Mr. Jefferson Davis, the President of the new confederacy, in his inaugural speech delivered on the 18th of February, declares that it is " an abuse of language " to call it " a revolution." Mr. Vice-President Stephens, on the contrary, in a speech at Savannah, on the 21st of March, pronounces it " one of the greatest revolutions in the annals of the world." The question is of great magnitude as one of constitutional and public law ; as one of morality it is of very little consequence whether the country is drenched in blood, in the exercise of a right claimed under the Constitution, or the right inherent in every community to revolt against an oppressive government. Unless the oppression is so extreme as to justify revolution, it would not justify the evil of breaking up a government,'under an abstract constitutional right to do so.

NEITHER A GRANTED NOR A RESERVED RIGHT.

This assumed right of Secession rests upon the doctrine that the Union is a compact between Independent States, from which any one of them may withdraw at pleasure in virtue of its sovereignty. This imaginary right has been the subject of discussion for more than thirty years, having been originally suggested, though not at first much dwelt upon, in connection with the kindred claim of a right, on the part of an individual State, to "nullify" an Act of Congress. It would, of course, be impossible within the limits of the hour to review these elaborate discussions. I will only remark, on this occasion, that none of the premises from which this remarkable conclusion is drawn, are recognized in the Constitution, and that the right of Secession, though claimed to be a " reserved " right, is not *expressly* reserved in it. That instrument does not purport to be a " compact," but a Constitution of Government. It appears, in its first sentence, not to have been entered into by the States, but to have been ordained and established by the People of the United States, for " themselves and their posterity." The States are not named in it ; nearly all the characteristic powers of sovereignty are expressly granted to the

* See Appendix A.

General Government and expressly prohibited to the States, and so far from reserving a right of secession to the latter, on any ground or under any pretence, it ordains and establishes in terms the Constitution of the United States as the Supreme Law of the land, any thing in the Constitution or Laws of any State to the contrary notwithstanding.

It would seem that this is as clear and positive as language can make it. But it is argued, that, though the right of secession is not reserved in terms, it must be considered as implied in the general reservation to the States and to the People of all the powers not granted to Congress nor prohibited to the States. This extraordinary assumption, more distinctly stated, is that, in direct defiance of the express grant to Congress and the express prohibition to the States of nearly all the powers of an independent government, there is, *by implication*, a right reserved to the States to assume and exercise all these powers thus vested in the Union and prohibited to themselves, simply in virtue of going through the ceremony of passing a law called an Ordinance of Secession. A general reservation to the States of powers not prohibited to them, nor granted to Congress is an implied reservation to the States of a right to exercise these very powers thus expressly delegated to Congress and thus expressly prohibited to the States !

The Constitution directs that the Congress of the United States shall have power to declare war, grant letters of marque and reprisal, to raise and support armies, to provide and maintain a navy, and that the President of the United States, by and with the advice and consent of the Senate, shall make treaties with foreign powers.

These express grants of power to the Government of the United States are followed by prohibitions as express to the several States :—

"No State shall enter into any treaty, alliance, or confederation, grant letters of marque or reprisal : no State shall, without the consent of Congress, lay any duty of tonnage, keep troops or ships of war in time of peace, enter into any agreement or compact with another State, or with a foreign power, or engage in war, unless actually invaded, or in such imminent danger as will not admit of delay."

These and numerous other express grants of power to the General Government, and express prohibitions to the States, are further enforced by the comprehensive provision, already recited, that the Constitution and Laws of the United States are paramount to the laws and Constitution of the separate States.

And this Constitution, with these express grants and express prohibitions, and with this express subordination of the States to the General Government, has been adopted by the People of all the States ; and all their judges and other officers, and all their citizens holding office under the government of the United States or the individual States, are solemnly sworn to support it.

In the face of all this, in defiance of all this, in violation of all this, in contempt of all this, the seceding States claim the right to exercise every power expressly delegated to Congress and expressly prohibited to the States by that Constitution, which every one of their prominent men, civil and military, is under oath to support. They have entered into a confederation, raised an army, attempted to provide a navy, issued letters of marque and reprisal, waged war, and that war,—Merciful Heaven forgive them,—not with a foreign enemy, not with the wild tribes which still desolate the unprotected frontier ; (they, it is said, are swelling, armed with tomahawk and scalping-knife, the Confederate forces ;) but with their own countrymen, and the mildest and most beneficent government on the face of the earth!

BEFORE THE REVOLUTION THE COLONIES WERE A PEOPLE.

But we are told all this is done in virtue of the Sovereignty of the States; as if, because a State is Sovereign, its people were incompetent to establish a government for themselves and their posterity. Certainly the States are clothed with Sovereignty for local purposes; but it is doubtful whether they ever possessed it in any other sense; and if they had, it is certain that they ceded it to the General Government, in adopting the Constitution. Before their independence of England was asserted, they constituted a provincial people. (Burke calls it "a glorious Empire,") subject to the British crown, organized for certain purposes under separate colonial charters, but, on some great occasions of political interest and public safety, acting as one. Thus they acted when, on the approach of the great Seven Years' War, which exerted such an important influence on the fate of British America, they sent their delegates to Albany to concert a plan of union. In the discussions of that plan which was reported by Franklin, the citizens of the colonies were evidently considered as a People. When the passage of the Stamp Act in 1765 roused the spirit of resistance throughout America, the Unity of her People assumed a still more practical form. "Union," says one of our great American historians,[*] "was the hope of Otis. Union that 'should knit and work into the very blood and bones of the original system every region as fast as settled.'" In this hope he argued against writs of assistance, and in this hope he brought about the call of the Convention at New York in 1765. At that Convention, the noble South Carolinian Christopher Gadsden, with prophetic foreboding of the disintegrating heresies of the present day, cautioned his associates against too great dependence on their colonial charters. "I wish," said he, "that the charters may not ensnare us at last, by drawing different Colonies to act differently in this great cause. Whenever that is the case all is over with the whole. *There ought to be no New England man, no New Yorker, known on the Continent, but all of us Americans.*"[†]

While the patriots in America counselled, and wrote, and spoke as a people, they were recognized as such in England. "Believe me," cried Colonel Barré in the House of Commons, "I this day told you so, the same spirit of Freedom which actuated *that People* at first will accompany them still. The people, I believe, are as truly loyal as any subjects the king has, but a People jealous of their liberties, and who will vindicate them, should they be violated."

When ten years later the great struggle long foreboded came on, it was felt, on both sides of the Atlantic, to be an attempt to reduce a free People beyond the sea to unconditional dependence on a parliament in which they were not represented. "What foundation have we," was the language of Chatham on the 27th Jan. 1775, "for our claims over America? What is our right to persist in such cruel and vindictive measures against *that loyal, respectable People?* How have this respectable people behaved under all their grievances? Repeal, therefore, I say. But bare repeal will not satisfy *this enlightened and spirited People.*" Lord Camden, in the same debate, exclaimed, "You have no right to tax America: the natural rights of man, and the immutable laws of Nature, are with *that People.*" Burke,

* Bancroft's History of the United States, vol. v., p. 292.   † Ibid., p. 365.

two months later, made his great speech for conciliation with America. "I do not know," he exclaimed, "the method of drawing up an indictment against a WHOLE PEOPLE." In a letter written two years after the commencement of the war, he traces the growth of the colonies from their feeble beginnings to the magnitude which they had attained when the revolution broke out, and in which his glowing imagination saw future grandeur and power beyond the reality. "At the first designation of these colonial assemblies," says he, "they were probably not intended for any thing more (nor perhaps did they think themselves much higher) than the municipal corporations within this island, to which some at present love to compare them. But nothing in progression can rest on its original plan; we may as well think of rocking a grown man in the cradle of an infant. Therefore, as the Colonies prospered and increased to A NUMEROUS AND MIGHTY PEOPLE, spreading over a very great tract of the globe, it was natural that they should attribute to assemblies so respectable in the formed Constitution, some part of the dignity of the great nations which they represented."

The meeting of the first Continental Congress of 1774 was the spontaneous impulse of the People. All their resolves and addresses proceed on the assumption that they represented a People. Their first appeal to the Royal authority was their letter to General Gage, remonstrating against the fortifications of Boston. "We entreat your Excellency to consider," they say, "what a tendency this conduct must have to irritate and force a *free People*, hitherto well disposed to peaceable measures, into hostilities." Their final act, at the close of the Session, their address to the King, one of the most eloquent and pathetic of State papers, appeals to him "in the name of all your Majesty's faithful People in America."

THE DECLARATION OF INDEPENDENCE RECOGNIZES A PEOPLE.

But this all-important principle in our political system is placed beyond doubt, by an authority which makes all further argument or illustration superfluous. That the citizens of the British Colonies, however divided for local purposes into different governments, when they ceased to be subject to the English crown, became *ipso facto* one People for all the high concerns of national existence, is a fact embodied in the Declaration of Independence itself. That august Manifesto, the *Magna Charta*, which introduced us into the family of nations, was issued to the world, so its first sentence sets forth—because "a decent respect for the opinions of mankind requires" such solemn announcement of motives and causes to be made, "when in the course of human events it becomes necessary for *one People* to dissolve the political bonds which have connected them with another." Mr. Jefferson Davis, in his message of the 29th of April, deems it important to remark, that, by the treaty of peace with Great Britain, "the several States were each by name recognized to be independent." It would be more accurate to say that the United States each by name were so recognized. Such enumeration was necessary, in order to fix beyond doubt, which of the Anglo-American colonies, twenty-five or six in number, were included in the recognition.* But it is surely a far more significant circumstance, that the separate States are not named in the Declaration

---

* Burke's account of "the English settlements in America," begins with Jamaica, and proceeds through the West India Islands. There were also English settlements on the Continent, Canada—and Nova Scotia,—which it was necessary to *exclude* from the Treaty, by an enumeration of the *included* Colonies.

of Independence, that they are called only by the collective designation of the
United States of America; that the manifesto is issued "in the name and by the
authority of the good people" of the Colonies, and that they are characterized in
the first sentence as "One People."

Let it not be thought that these are the latitudinarian doctrines of modern
times, or of a section of the country predisposed to a loose construction of laws
and Constitutions. Listen, I pray you, to the noble words of a Southern revolutionary patriot and statesman :—

"The separate independence and individual sovereignty of the several States
were never thought of by the enlightened band of patriots who framed the Declaration of Independence. The several States are not even mentioned by name in any
part of it, as if it was intended to impress this maxim on America, that our Freedom
and Independence arose from our Union, and that without it we could neither be
free nor independent. Let us then consider all attempts to weaken this Union, by
maintaining that each State is separately and individually independent, as a species
of political heresy, which can never benefit us, and may bring on us the most
serious distresses."* These are the solemn and prophetic words of Charles Cotes-
worth Pinckney; the patriot, the soldier, the statesman; the trusted friend of
Washington, repeatedly called by him to the highest offices of the Government;
the one name that stands highest and brightest, on the list of the great men of
South Carolina.†

THE ARTICLES OF CONFEDERATION.

Not only was the Declaration of Independence made in the name of the one
People of the United States, but the war by which it was sustained was carried on
by their authority. A very grave historical error, in this respect, is often committed by the politicians of the Secession School. Mr. Davis, in his message of
the 29th of April, having called the old Confederation "a close alliance," says :
"under this contract of alliance the war of the revolution was successfully waged,
and resulted in the treaty of peace with Great Britain of 1783, by the terms of
which the several States were each by name recognized to be independent." I have
already given the reason for this enumeration, but the main fact alleged in the
passage is entirely without foundation. The Articles of Confederation were first
signed by the delegates from eight of the States, on the 9th of July, 1778, more
than three years after the commencement of the war, long after the capitulation
of Burgoyne, the alliance with France, and the reception of a French Minister.
The ratification of the other States was given at intervals the following years, the
last not till 1781, seven months only before the virtual close of the war, by the
surrender of Cornwallis. Then, and not till then, was "the Contract of Alliance"
consummated. Most true it is, as Mr. Davis bids us remark, that, by these Articles of Confederation the States retained "each its sovereignty, freedom, and independence." It is not less true, that their selfish struggle to exercise and enforce
their assumed rights as separate sovereignties was the source of the greatest diffi-
culties and dangers of the Revolution, and risked its success; not less true, that most
of the great powers of a sovereign State were nominally conferred even by these

* Elliott's Debates, vol. iv., p. 301.
† See an admirable sketch of his character in Trescot's Diplomatic History of the Administrations of Washington and Adams, pp. 169—171.

articles on the Congress, and that that body was regarded and spoken of by Washington himself as THE "SOVEREIGN OF THE UNION." *

But feeble as the old Confederation was, and distinctly as it recognized the sovereignty of the States, it recognized in them no right to withdraw at their pleasure from the Union. On the contrary, it was specially provided that "the Articles of Confederation should be inviolably preserved by every State," and that "the Union should be perpetual." It is true that in a few years, from the inherent weakness of the central power, and from the want of means to enforce its authority on the individual citizen, it fell to pieces. It sickened and died from the poison of what General Pinckney aptly called "the heresy of State Sovereignty," and in its place a Constitution was ordained and established "in order to form a more perfect Union;" a Union more binding on its members than this "contract of alliance," which yet was to be "inviolably observed by every State;" more durable than the old Union, which yet was declared to be "perpetual." This great and beneficent change was a Revolution—happily a peaceful revolution, the most important change probably ever brought about in a government, without bloodshed. The new government was unanimously adopted by all the members of the old Confederation, by some more promptly than by others, but by all within the space of four years.

THE STATES MIGHT BE COERCED UNDER THE CONFEDERATION.

Much has been said against *coercion*, that is, the employment of force to compel obedience to the laws of the United States, when they are resisted under the assumed authority of a State; but even the old Confederation, with all its weakness, in the opinion of the most eminent contemporary statesmen possessed this power. Great stress is laid by politicians of the Secession School on the fact, that in a project for amending the articles of Confederation brought forward by Judge Paterson in the Federal Convention, it was proposed to clothe the Government with this power and the proposal was not adopted. This is a very inaccurate statement of the facts of the case. The proposal formed part of a project which was rejected *in toto*. The reason why this power of State coercion was not granted *eo nomine*, in the new Constitution, is that it was wholly superfluous and inconsistent with the fundamental principle of the Government. Within the sphere of its delegated powers, the General Government deals with the individual citizen. If its power is resisted, the person or persons resisting it do so at their peril and are amenable to the law. They can derive no immunity from State Legislatures or State Conventions, because the Constitution and laws of the United States are the Supreme Law of the Land. If the resistance assumes an organized form, on the part of numbers too great to be restrained by the ordinary powers of the law, it is then an insurrection, which the General Government is expressly authorized to suppress. Did any one imagine in 1793, when General Washington called out 15,000 men to suppress the insurrection in the Western counties of Pennsylvania, that if the insurgents had happened to have the control of a majority of the Legislature, and had thus been able to clothe their rebellion with a pretended form of law, that he would have been obliged to disband his troops, and return himself baffled and discomfited to Mount Vernon? If John Brown's raid at Harper's Ferry, instead of being the

---

* Sparks' Washington. vol. ix., pp. 12, 23, 29.

project of one misguided individual and a dozen and a half deluded followers, had been the organized movement of the States of Ohio and Pennsylvania, do the Seceders hold that the United States would have had no right to protect Virginia, or punish the individuals concerned in her invasion? Do the seceding States really mean, after all, to deny, that if a State law is passed to prevent the rendition of a fugitive slave, the General Government has any right to employ force to effect his surrender?

But, as I have said, even the old Confederation, with all its weakness, was held by the ablest contemporary statesmen, and that of the State rights school, to possess the power of enforcing its requisitions against a delinquent State. Mr. Jefferson, in a letter to Mr. Adams of the 11th of July, 1786, on the subject of providing a naval force of 150 guns to chastise the Barbary Powers, urges, as an additional reason for such a step, that it would arm " the Federal head with the safest of all the instruments of coercion, over its delinquent members, and prevent it from using what would be less safe," viz.: a land force. Writing on the same subject to Mr. Monroe a month later, (11 Aug. 1786.) he answers the objection of expense thus : " It will be said, ' There is no money in the Treasury.' There never will be money in the Treasury till the Confederacy shows its teeth. *The States must see the rod, perhaps it must be felt by some of them.* Every rational citizen must wish to see an effective instrument of coercion, and should fear to see it on any other element than the water. A naval force can never endanger our liberties nor occasion bloodshed ; a land force would do both." In the following year, and when the Confederation was at its last gasp, Mr. Jefferson was still of the opinion that it possessed the power of coercing the States, and that it was expedient to exercise it. In a letter to Col. Carrington of the 4th of April, 1787, he says: " It has been so often said as to be generally believed, that Congress have no power by the Confederation to enforce any thing, for instance, contributions of money. It was not necessary to give them that power expressly, they have it by the law of nature. *When two parties make a compact, there results to each the power of compelling the other to execute it.* Compulsion was never so easy as in our case, when a single frigate would soon levy on the commerce of a single State the deficiency of its contributions."

Such was Mr. Jefferson's opinion of the powers of Congress, under the " old contract of alliance." Will any reasonable man maintain that under a constitution of government there can be less power to enforce the laws?

STATE SOVEREIGNTY DOES NOT AUTHORIZE SECESSION.

But the cause of secession gains nothing by magnifying the doctrine of the Sovereignty of the States or calling the Constitution a compact between them. Calling it a compact does not change a word of its text, and no theory of what is implied in the word " Sovereignty " is of any weight, in opposition to the actual provisions of the instrument itself. *Sovereignty* is a word of very various signification. It is one thing in China, another in Turkey, another in Russia, another in France, another in England, another in Switzerland, another in San Marino, another in the individual American States, and it is something different from all in the United States. To maintain that, because the State of Virginia, for instance, was in some sense or other a sovereign State, when her people adopted the Federal Constitution, (which in terms was ordained and established not only for the people of that day, but for their posterity,) she may therefore at pleasure secede from the Union existing under that Constitution, is simply to beg the question. That question is not what was the theory or form of government existing in Virginia, before the Constitution, but what are the provisions of the Constitution which her people adopted and made their own? Does the Constitution of the United States permit or forbid the States to enter into a confederation? Is it a mere loose partnership, which any of the parties can break up at pleasure, or is it a Constitution of government, delegating to Congress and prohibiting to the States most of the primal functions of a sovereign power;—Peace, War, Commerce, Finance, Navy, Army, Mail, Mint; Executive, Legislative, and Judicial functions? The States are not named in it; the word Sovereignty does not occur in it; the right of secession is as much ignored in it as the precession of the Equinoxes, and all the great prerogatives which characterize an independent member of the family of nations are by distinct grant conferred on Congress by the People of the United States and prohibited to the individual States of the Union. Is it not the height of absurdity to maintain that all these express grants and distinct prohibitions, and constitutional arrangements, may be set at nought by an individual State under the pretence that she was a sovereign State before she assented to or ratified them; in other words, that an act is of no binding force because it was performed by an authorized and competent agent?

In fact, to deduce from the sovereignty of the States the right of seceding from the Union is the most stupendous *non sequitur* that was ever advanced in grave affairs. The only legitimate inference to be drawn from that sovereignty is precisely the reverse. If any one right can be predicated of a sovereign State, it is that of forming or adopting a frame of government. She may do it alone, or she may do it as a member of a Union. She may enter into a loose pact for ten years or till a partisan majority of a convention, goaded on by ambitious aspirants to power, shall vote in secret session to dissolve it; or she may, after grave deliberation and mature counsel, led by the wisest and most virtuous of the land, ratify and adopt a constitution of government, ordained and established not only for that generation, but their posterity, subject only to the inalienable right of revolution possessed by every political community.

What would be thought in private affairs of a man who should seriously claim the right to revoke a grant, in consequence of having an unqualified right to make it? A right to break a contract, because he had a right to enter into it? To what extent is it more rational on the part of a State to found the right to dissolve the Union on the competence of the parties to form it; the right to prostrate a government on the fact that it was constitutionally framed?

PARALLEL CASES: IRELAND, SCOTLAND.

But let us look at parallel cases, and they are by no means wanting. In the year 1800, a union was formed between England and Ireland. Ireland, before she entered into the union, was subject, indeed, to the English crown, but she had her own parliament, consisting of her own Lords and Commons, and enacting her own laws. In 1800 she entered into a constitutional union with England on the basis of articles of agreement, jointly accepted by the two parliaments.* The union was

* Annual Register, xlii., p. 190

opposed at the time by a powerful minority in Ireland, and Mr. O'Connell succeeded, thirty years later, by ardent appeals to the sensibilities of the people, in producing an almost unanimous desire for its dissolution. He professed, however, although he had wrought his countrymen to the verge of rebellion, to aim at nothing but a constitutional repeal of the articles of union by the parliament of Great Britain. It never occurred even to his fervid imagination, that, because Ireland was an independent government when she entered into the union, it was competent for her at her discretion to secede from it. What would our English friends, who have learned from our Secessionists the " inherent right " of a disaffected State to secede from our Union, have thought, had Mr. O'Connell, in the paroxysms of his agitation, claimed the right on the part of Ireland, by her own act, to sever her union with England ?

Again, in 1706, Scotland and England formed a Constitutional Union. They also, though subject to the same monarch, were in other respects Sovereign and independent Kingdoms. They had each its separate parliament, courts of justice, laws, and established national church. Articles of union were established between them ; but all the laws and statutes of either kingdom not contrary to these articles, remained in force.* A powerful minority in Scotland disapproved of the Union at the time. Nine years afterward an insurrection broke out in Scotland under a prince, who claimed to be the lawful, as he certainly was the lineal, heir to the throne. The rebellion was crushed, but the disaffection in which it had its origin was not wholly appeased. In thirty years more a second Scottish insurrection took place, and, as before, under the lead of the lineal heir to the crown. On neither occasion that I ever heard of, did it enter into the imagination of rebel or loyalist, that Scotland was acting under a reserved right as a sovereign kingdom, to secede from the Union, or that the movement was any thing less than an insurrection ; revolution if it succeeded ; treason and rebellion if it failed. Neither do I recollect that, in less than a month after either insurrection broke out, any one of the friendly and neutral powers made haste, in anticipation even of the arrival of the ministers of the reigning sovereign, to announce that the rebels " would be recognized as belligerents."

VIRGINIA VAINLY ATTEMPTS TO ESTABLISH A RESERVED RIGHT.

In fact, it is so plain, in the nature of things, that there can be no constitutional right to break up a government unless it is expressly provided for, that the politicians of the secession school are driven back, at every turn, to a *reserved* right. I have already shown that there is no such *express* reservation, and I have dwelt on the absurdity of getting by *implication* a reserved right to violate every *express* provision of a constitution. In this strait, Virginia, proverbially skilled in logical subtilties, has attempted to find an express reservation, not, of course, in the Constitution itself, where it does not exist, but in her original act of adhesion, or rather in the declaration of the " impressions " under which that act was adopted. The ratification itself of Virginia, was positive and unconditional. " We, the said delegates, in the name and behalf of *the People of Virginia*, do, by these presents, assent and ratify the Constitution recommended on the 17th day of September, 1787, by the Federal Convention, *for the government of the United States,* hereby announcing

---

* Rapin's History of England, vol. iv., p. 741-6.

to all those whom it may concern, that the said Constitution is binding upon the said *People*, according to an authentic copy hereunto annexed. Done in Convention this 26th day of June, 1788."

This, as you perceive, is an absolute and unconditional ratification of the Constitution by the People of Virginia. An attempt, however, is made, by the late Convention in Virginia, in their ordinance of secession, to extract a reservation of a right to secede, out of the declaration contained in the preamble to the act of ratification. That preamble declares it to be an "impression" of the people of Virginia, that the powers granted under the Constitution, being derived from the people of the United States, may be resumed BY THEM, whenever the same shall be perverted to their injury or oppression. The ordinance of secession passed by the recent convention, purporting to cite this declaration, omits the words *by them*, that is, by the People of the United States, not by the people of any single State, thus arrogating to the people of Virginia alone what the Convention of 1788 claimed only, and that by way of "impression," for the People of the United States.

By this most grave omission of the vital words of the sentence, the Convention, I fear, intended to lead the incautious or the ignorant to the conclusion, that the Convention of 1788 asserted the right of an individual State to resume the powers granted in the Constitution to the General Government; a claim for which there is not the slightest foundation in Constitutional history. On the contrary, when the ill-omened doctrine of State nullification was sought to be sustained by the same argument in 1830, and the famous Virginia resolutions of 1798 were appealed to by Mr. Calhoun and his friends, as affording countenance to that doctrine, it was repeatedly and emphatically declared by Mr. Madison, the author of the resolutions, that they were intended to claim, not for an individual State, but for the United States, by whom the Constitution was ordained and established, the right of remedying its abuses by constitutional ways, such as united protest, repeal, or an amendment of the Constitution.* Incidentally to the discussion of nullification, he denied over and over again the right of peaceable secession; and this fact was well known to some of the members of the late Convention at Richmond. When the secrets of their assembly are laid open, no doubt it will appear that there were some faithful Abdiels to proclaim the fact. Oh, that the venerable sage, second to none of his patriot compeers in framing the Constitution, the equal associate of Hamilton in recommending it to the People; its great champion in the Virginia Convention of 1788, and its faithful vindicator in 1830, against the deleterious heresy of nullification, could have been spared to protect it, at the present day, from the still deadlier venom of Secession! But he is gone; the principles, the traditions, and the illustrious memories which gave to Virginia her name and her praise in the land, are no longer cherished; the work of Washington, and Madison, and Randolph, and Pendleton, and Marshall is repudiated, and nullifiers, precipitators, and seceders gather in secret conclave to destroy the Constitution, in the very building that holds the monumental statue of the Father of his Country!

THE VIRGINIA RESOLUTIONS OF 1798.

Having had occasion to allude to the Virginia resolutions of 1798, I may observe that of these famous resolves, the subject of so much political romance, it is

* Maguire's Collection, p. 213.

time that a little plain truth should be promulgated. The country, in 1798, was vehemently agitated by the struggles of the domestic parties, which about equally divided it, and these struggles were urged to unwonted and extreme bitterness, by the preparations made and making for a war with France. By an act of Congress, passed in the summer of that year, the President of the United States was clothed with power to send from the country any alien whom he might judge dangerous to the public peace and safety, or who should be concerned in any treasonable or secret machinations against the Government of the United States. This act was passed as a war measure; it was to be in force two years, and it expired by its own limitation on the 25th of June, 1800. War, it is true, had not been formally declared; but hostilities on the ocean had taken place on both sides, and the army of the United States had been placed upon a war footing. The measure was certainly within the war power, and one which no prudent commander, even without the authority of a statute, would hesitate to execute in an urgent case within his own district. Congress thought fit to provide for and regulate its exercise by law.

Two or three weeks later (14th July, 1798) another law was enacted, making it penal to combine or conspire with intent to oppose any lawful measure of the Government of the United States, or to write, print, or publish any false and scandalous writing against the Government, either House of Congress, or the President of the United States. In prosecutions under this law, it was provided that the Truth might be pleaded in justification, and that the Jury should be judges of the law as well as of the fact. This law was by its own limitation to expire at the close of the then current Presidential term.

Such are the famous alien and sedition laws, passed under the Administration of that noble and true-hearted revolutionary patriot, John Adams, though not recommended by him officially or privately; adjudged to be constitutional by the Supreme Court of the United States; distinctly approved by Washington, Patrick Henry, and Marshall; and, whatever else may be said of them, certainly preferable to the laws which, throughout the Seceding States, Judge Lynch would not fail to enforce at the lamp-post and tar-bucket against any person guilty of the offences against which these statutes were aimed.

It suited, however, the purposes of party at that time, to raise a formidable clamor against these laws. It was in vain that their Constitutionality was affirmed by the Judiciary of the United States. "Nothing," said Washington, alluding to these laws, "will produce the least change in the conduct of the leaders of the opposition to the measures of the General Government. They have points to carry from which no reasoning, no inconsistency of conduct, no absurdity can divert them." Such, in the opinion of Washington, was the object for which the Legislatures of Virginia and Kentucky passed their famous resolutions of 1798, the former drafted by Mr. Madison, and the latter by Mr. Jefferson, and sent to a friend in Kentucky to be brought forward. These resolutions were transmitted to the other States for their concurrence. The replies from the States which made any response were referred the following year to committees in Virginia and Kentucky. In the Legislature of Virginia, an elaborate report was made by Mr. Madison, explaining and defending the resolutions; in Kentucky another resolve reaffirming those of the preceding year was drafted by Mr. Wilson Cary Nicholas, not by Mr. Jefferson, as stated by General McDuffie. Our respect for the distinguished men who took the lead on this occasion, then ardently engaged in the warfare of politics, must not make us fear to tell the truth, that the simple object of the entire movement was to make " political capital " for the approaching election, by holding up to the excited imaginations of the masses the Alien and Sedition laws, as an infraction of the Constitution, which threatened the overthrow of the liberties of the People. The resolutions maintained that, the States being parties to the Constitutional compact, in a case of deliberate, palpable, and dangerous exercise of powers not granted by the compact, the States have a right and are in duty bound to *interpose* for preventing the progress of the evil.

Such, in brief, was the main purport of the Virginia and Kentucky resolutions. The sort of interposition intended was left in studied obscurity. Not a word was dropped of secession from the Union. Mr. Nicholas's resolution in 1799 hinted at " nullification " as the appropriate remedy for an unconstitutional law, but what was meant by the ill-sounding word was not explained. The words " null, void, and of no effect," contained in the original draft of the Virginia resolutions, were, on motion of John Taylor of Caroline, stricken from them, on their passage through the assembly ; and Mr. Madison, in his report of 1799, carefully explains that no extra constitutional measures were intended. One of the Kentucky resolutions ends with an invitation to the States to unite in a petition to Congress to repeal the laws.

These resolutions were communicated, as I have said, to the other States for concurrence. From most of them no response was received : some adopted dissenting reports and resolutions ; NOT ONE CONCURRED. But the resolutions did their work—all that they were intended or expected to do—by shaking the Administration. At the ensuing election, Mr. Jefferson, at whose instance the entire movement was made, was chosen President by a very small majority ; Mr. Madison was placed at the head of his administration as Secretary of State ; the obnoxious laws expired by their own limitation ; not repealed by the dominant party, as Mr. Calhoun with strange inadvertence asserts ; * and Mr. Jefferson proceeded to administer the Government upon constitutional principles quite as lax, to say the least, as those of his predecessors. If there was any marked departure in his general policy from the course hitherto pursued, it was that, having some theoretical prejudices against a navy, he allowed that branch of the service to languish. By no Administration have the powers of the General Government been more liberally construed—not to say further strained—sometimes beneficially, as in the acquisition of Louisiana, sometimes perniciously as in the embargo. The resolutions of 1798, and the metaphysics they inculcated, were surrendered to the cobwebs which habitually await the plausible exaggerations of the canvass after an election is decided. These resolutions of 1798 have been sometimes in Virginia waked from their slumbers at closely contested elections as a party cry ; the report of the Hartford Convention, without citing them by name, borrows their language ; but as representing in their modern interpretation any system on which the Government ever was or could be administered, they were buried in the same grave as the Laws which called them forth.

Unhappily during their transient vitality, like the butterfly which deposits its egg in the apple blossoms that have so lately filled our orchards with beauty and

* Mr. Calhoun's Discourse on the Constitution, p. 859.

perfume—a gilded harmless moth, whose food is a dew drop, whose life is a midsummer's day—these resolutions, misconceived and perverted, proved, in the minds of ambitious and reckless politicians, the germ of a fatal heresy. The butterfly's egg is a microscopic speck, but as the fruit grows, the little speck gives life to a greedy and nauseous worm, that gnaws and bores to the heart of the apple, and renders it, though smooth and fair without, foul and bitter and rotten within. In like manner, the theoretical generalities of these resolutions, intending nothing in the minds of their authors but constitutional efforts to procure the repeal of obnoxious laws, matured in the minds of a later generation into the deadly paradoxes of 1830 and 1860—kindred products of the same soil, *venenorum ferax;*— the one asserting the monstrous absurdity that a State, though remaining in the Union, could by her single act nullify a law of Congress; the other teaching the still more preposterous doctrine, that a single State may nullify the Constitution. The first of these heresies failed to spread far beyond the latitude where it was engendered. In the Senate of the United States, the great acuteness of its inventor, (Mr. Calhoun,) then the Vice-President, and the accomplished rhetoric of its champion, (Mr. Hayne,) failed to raise it above the level of a plausible sophism. It sunk forever discredited beneath the sturdy common sense and indomitable will of Jackson, the mature wisdom of Livingston, the keen analysis of Clay, and the crushing logic of Webster.

Nor was this all: the venerable author of the Resolutions of 1798 and of the report of 1799 was still living in a green old age. His connection with those State papers and still more his large participation in the formation and adoption of the Constitution, entitled him, beyond all men living, to be consulted on the subject. No effort was spared by the Leaders of the Nullification school to draw from him even a qualified assent to their theories. But in vain. He not only refused to admit their soundness, but he devoted his time and energies for three laborious years to the preparation of essays and letters, of which the object was to demonstrate that his resolutions and report did not, and could not bear the Carolina interpretation. He earnestly maintained that the separate action of an individual State was not contemplated by them, and that they had in view nothing but the concerted action of the States to procure the repeal of unconstitutional laws or an amendment of the Constitution.*

With one such letter written with this intent, I was myself honored. It filled ten pages of the journal in which with his permission it was published. It unfolded the true theory of the Constitution and the meaning and design of the resolutions, and exposed the false gloss attempted to be placed upon them by the Nullifiers, with a clearness and force of reasoning which defied refutation. None, to my knowledge, was ever attempted. The politicians of the Nullification and Secession school, as far as I am aware, have from that day to this made no attempt to grapple with Mr. Madison's letter of August, 1830.† Mr. Calhoun certainly made no such attempt in the elaborate treatise composed by him, mainly for the purpose of expounding the doctrine of nullification. He claims the support of these resolutions, without adverting to the fact that his interpretation of them had been repudiated

* A very considerable portion of the important volume containing a selection from the Madison papers, and printed "exclusively for private distribution" by J. C. McGuire, Esq., in 1853, is taken up with these letters and essays.

† North American Review, vol. xxxi., p. 537.

by their illustrious author. He repeats his exploded paradoxes as confidently, as if Mr. Madison himself had expired with the Alien and Sedition laws, and left no testimony to the meaning of his resolutions ; while, at the present day, with equal confidence, the same resolutions are appealed to by the disciples of Mr. Calhoun as sustaining the doctrine of secession, in the face of the positive declaration of their author, when that doctrine first began to be broached, that they will bear no such interpretation.

MR. CALHOUN DID NOT CLAIM A CONSTITUTIONAL RIGHT OF SECESSION.

In this respect the disciples have gone beyond the master. There is a single sentence in Mr. Calhoun's elaborate volume in which he maintains the right of a State to secede from the Union. (Page 301.) There is reason to suppose, however, that he intended to claim only the inalienable right of revolution. In 1828, a declaration of political principles was drawn up by him for the State of South Carolina, in which it was expressly taught, that the people of that State by adopting the Federal Constitution had "modified *its original right of sovereignty*, whereby its individual consent was necessary to any change in its political condition, and by becoming a member of the Union, had placed that power in the hands of three-fourths of the States, [the number necessary for a Constitutional amendment,] in whom the highest power known to the Constitution actually resides." In a recent patriotic speech of Mr. Reverdy Johnson, at Frederick, Md., on the 7th of May, the distinct authority of Mr. Calhoun is quoted as late as 1844 against the right of separate action on the part of an individual State, and I am assured by the same respected gentleman, that it is within his personal knowledge, that Mr. Calhoun did not maintain the peaceful right of secession.*

SECESSION AS A REVOLUTION.

But it may be thought a waste of time to argue against a Constitutional right of peaceful Secession, since no one denies the right of Revolution ; and no pains are spared by the disaffected leaders, while they claim indeed the Constitutional right, to represent their movement as the uprising of an indignant People against an oppressive and tyrannical Government.

IS THE GOVERNMENT OF THE UNITED STATES OPPRESSIVE AND TYRANNICAL?

An oppressive and tyrannical government! Let us examine this pretence for a few moments, first in the general, and then in the detail of its alleged tyrannies and abuses.

This oppressive and tyrannical Government is the successful solution of a problem, which had tasked the sagacity of mankind from the dawn of civilization : viz. : to find a form of polity, by which institutions purely popular could be extended over a vast empire, free alike from despotic centralization and undue preponderance of the local powers. It was necessarily a complex system ; a Union at once federal and national. It leaves to the separate States the control of all matters of purely local administration, and confides to the central power the management of Foreign affairs and of all other concerns in which the United family have a joint interest. All the organized and delegated powers depend directly or very nearly

* See Appendix B.

so on popular choice. This Government was not imposed upon the People by a foreign conqueror; it is not an inheritance descending from barbarous ages, laden with traditionary abuses, which create a painful ever-recurring necessity of reform; it is not the conceit of heated enthusiasts in the spasms of a revolution. It is the recent and voluntary frame-work of an enlightened age, compacted by wise and good men, with deliberation and care, working upon materials prepared by long Colonial discipline. In framing it, they sought to combine the merits and to avoid the defects of former systems of government. The greatest possible liberty of the citizen is the basis; just representation the ruling principle, reconciling with rare ingenuity the federal equality of the States, with the proportionate influence of numbers. Its legislative and executive magistrates are freely chosen at short periods; its judiciary alone holding office by a more permanent, but still sufficiently responsible, tenure. No money flows into or out of the Treasury but under the direct sanction of the representatives of the People, on whom also all the great functions of Government for peace and war, within the limits already indicated, are devolved. No hereditary titles or privileges, no distinction of ranks, no established church, no courts of high commission, no censorship of the press, are known to the system; not a drop of blood has ever flowed under its authority for a political offence; but this tyrannical and oppressive Government has certainly exhibited a more perfect development of equal republican principles, than has ever before existed on any considerable scale. Under its benign influence, the country, every part of the country, has prospered beyond all former example. Its population has increased; its commerce, agriculture, and manufactures have flourished; manners, arts, education, letters, all that dignifies and ennobles man, have in a shorter period attained a higher point of cultivation than has ever before been witnessed in a newly settled region. The consequence has been consideration and influence abroad and marvellous well-being at home. The world has looked with admiration upon the Country's progress; we have ourselves contemplated it, perhaps, with undue self-complacency. Armies without conscription; navies without impressment, and neither army nor navy swelled to an oppressive size; an over-flowing treasury without direct taxation or oppressive taxation of any kind; churches without number and with no denominational preferences on the part of the State; schools and colleges accessible to all the people; a free and a cheap press; —all the great institutions of social life extending their benefits to the mass of the community. Such, no one can deny, is the general character of this oppressive and tyrannical government.

But perhaps this Government, however wisely planned, however beneficial even in its operation, may have been rendered distasteful, or may have become oppressive in one part of the country and to one portion of the people, in consequence of the control of affairs having been monopolized or unequally shared by another portion. In a Confederacy, the people of one section are not well pleased to be even mildly governed by an exclusive domination of the other. In point of fact this is the allegation, the persistent allegation of the South, that from the foundation of the Government it has been wielded by the people of the North for their special, often exclusive, benefit, and to the injury and oppression of the South. Let us see. Out of seventy-two years since the organization of the Government, the Executive chair has, for sixty-four years, been filled nearly all the time by Southern

Presidents; and when that was not the case, by Presidents possessing the confidence of the South. For a still longer period, the controlling influences of the Legislative and Judicial departments of the Government have centred in the same quarter. Of all the offices in the gift of the central power in every department, far more than her proportionate share has always been enjoyed by the South. She is at this moment revolting against a Government, not only admitted to be the mildest and most beneficent ever organized this side Utopia, but one of which she has herself from the first, almost monopolized the administration.

CAUSE OF THE REVOLUTION ALLEGED BY SOUTH CAROLINA.

But are there no wrongs, abuses, and oppressions, alleged to have been suffered by the South, which have rendered her longer submission to the Federal Government intolerable, and which are pleaded as the motive and justification of the revolt? Of course there are, but with such variation and uncertainty of statement as to render their examination difficult. The manifesto of South Carolina of the 20th of Dec. last, which led the way in this inauspicious movement, sets forth nothing but the passage of State laws to obstruct the surrender of fugitive slaves. The document does not state that South Carolina herself ever lost a slave in consequence of these laws, it is not probable she ever did, and yet she makes the existence of these laws, which are wholly inoperative as far as she is concerned, and which probably never caused to the entire South the loss of a dozen fugitives, the ground for breaking up the Union and plunging the country into a civil war. But I shall presently revert to this topic.

Other statements in other quarters enlarge the list of grievances. In the month of November last, after the result of the presidential election was ascertained, a very interesting discussion of the subject of secession took place at Milledgeville, before the members of the Legislature of Georgia and the citizens generally, between two gentlemen of great ability and eminence, since elected, the one Secretary of State, the other Vice-President of the new Confederacy; the former urging the necessity and duty of immediate secession;—the latter opposing it. I take the grievances and abuses of the Federal Government, which the South has suffered at the hands of the North, and which were urged by the former speaker as the grounds of secession, as I find them stated and to some extent answered by his friend and fellow-citizen (then opposed to secession) according to the report in the Milledgeville papers.

CAUSES ALLEGED BY GEORGIA: THE FISHING BOUNTIES.

And what, think you, was the grievance in the front rank of those oppressions on the part of the North, which have driven the long-suffering and patient South to open rebellion against "the best Government that the history of the world gives any account of"? It was not that upon which the Convention of South Carolina relied. You will hardly believe it; posterity will surely not believe it. "We listened," said Mr. Vice-President Stephens, in his reply, "to my honorable friend last night, (Mr. Toombs,) as he recounted the evils of this Government. *The first was the fishing bounties paid mostly to the sailors of New England.*" The bounty paid by the Federal Government to encourage the deep-sea fisheries of the United States!

You are aware that this laborious branch of industry has, by all maritime States, been ever regarded with special favor as the nursery of naval power. The fisheries of the American colonies before the American Revolution drew from Burke one of the most gorgeous bursts of eloquence in our language,—in any language. They were all but annihilated by the Revolution, but they furnished the men who followed Manly, and Tucker, and Biddle, and Paul Jones to the jaws of death. Reviving after the war, they attracted the notice of the First Congress, and were recommended to their favor by Mr. Jefferson, then Secretary of State. This favor was at first extended to them in the shape of a draw-back of the duty on the various imported articles employed in the building and outfit of the vessels and on the foreign salt used in preserving the fish. The complexity of this arrangement led to the substitution at first of a certain bounty on the quantity of the fish exported; afterwards on the tonnage of the vessels employed in the fisheries. All administrations have concurred in the measure; Presidents of all parties,—though there has not been much variety of party in that office,—have approved the appropriations. If the North had a local interest in these bounties, the South got the principal food of her laboring population so much the cheaper; and she had her common share in the protection which the navy afforded her coasts, and in the glory which it shed on the flag of the country. But since, unfortunately, the deep-sea fisheries do not exist in the Gulf of Mexico, nor, as in the "age of Pyrrha," on the top of the Blue Ridge, it has been discovered of late years that these bounties are a violation of the Constitution; a largess bestowed by the common treasury on one section of the country, and not shared by the other; one of the hundred ways, in a word, in which the rapacious North is fattening upon the oppressed and pillaged South. You will naturally wish to know the amount of this tyrannical and oppressive bounty. It is stated by a senator from Alabama (Mr. Clay) who has warred against it with perseverance and zeal, and succeeded in the last Congress in carrying a bill through the Senate for its repeal, to have amounted, on the average, to an annual sum of 200,005 dollars! Such is the portentous grievance which in Georgia stands at the head of the acts of oppression, for which, although repealed in one branch of Congress, the Union is to be broken up, and the country desolated by war. Switzerland revolted because an Austrian tyrant invaded the sanctity of her firesides, crushed out the eyes of aged patriots, and compelled her fathers to shoot apples from the heads of her sons; the Low Countries revolted against the fires of the Inquisition, and the infernal cruelties of Alva; our fathers revolted because they were taxed by a parliament in which they were not represented; the Cotton States revolt because a paltry subvention is paid to the hardy fishermen who form the nerve and muscle of the American Navy.

But it is not, we shall be told, the amount of the bounty, but the principle, as our fathers revolted against a three-penny tax on tea. But that was because it was laid by a parliament in which the Colonies were not represented, and which yet claimed the right to bind them in all cases. The Fishing Bounty is bestowed by a Government which has been from the first controlled by the South. Then how unreasonable to expect or to wish, that, in a country so vast as ours, no public expenditure should be made for the immediate benefit of one part or one interest that cannot be identically repeated in every other. A liberal policy, or rather the necessity of the case, demands, that what the public good, upon the whole, requires,

should under constitutional limitations be done where it is required, offsetting the
local benefit which may accrue from the expenditure made in one place and for one
object, with the local benefit from the same source, in some other place for some other
object. More money was expended by the United States in removing the Indians
from Georgia, eight or ten times as much was expended for the same object in Florida,
as has been paid for Fishing Bounties in seventy years. For the last year, to pay
for the expense of the post-office in the seceding States, and enable our fellow-citizens there to enjoy the comforts of a newspaper and letter mail to the same
extent as they are enjoyed in the other States, three millions of dollars were
paid from the common Treasury. The post-office bounty paid to the seceding
States exceeded seventeen fold the annual average amount of the Fishing Bounty
paid to the North. In four years that excess would equal the sum total of the
amount paid since 1792 in bounties to the deep-sea fishery! This circumstance
probably explains the fact, that the pride of the Southern Confederacy was not
alarmed at having the mails still conveyed by the United States, three or four
months after the forts had been seized, the arsenals emptied, and the mints plundered.

NAVIGATION LAWS.

The second of the grievances under which the South is laboring, and which, according to Mr. Stephens, was on the occasion alluded to pleaded by the Secretary
of State of the new Confederacy as a ground for dissolving the Union, is the Navigation Laws, which give to American vessels the exclusive enjoyment of our own
coasting trade. This also is a policy coeval with the Government of the United
States, and universally adopted by maritime powers, though relaxed by England
within the last few years. Like the fishing bounty, it is a policy adopted for the
purpose of fostering the commercial and with that the naval marine of the United
States. All administrations of all parties have favored it; under its influence our
commercial tonnage has grown up to be second to no other in the world, and our
navy has proved itself adequate to all the exigencies of peace and war. And are
these no objects in a national point of view? Are the seceding politicians really
insensible to interests of such paramount national importance? Can they, for the
sake of an imaginary infinitesimal reduction of coastwise freights, be willing to run
even the risk of impairing our naval prosperity? Are they insensible to the fact
that nothing but the growth of the American commercial marine protects the entire
freighting interest of the country, in which the South is more deeply interested than
the North, from European monopoly? The South did not always take so narrow
a view of the subject. When the Constitution was framed, and the American Merchant Marine was inconsiderable, the discrimination in favor of United States vessels, which then extended to the foreign trade, was an object of some apprehension
on the part of the planting States. But there were statesmen in the South at that
day, who did not regard the shipping interest as a local concern. "So far," said
Mr. Edward Rutledge, in the South Carolina Convention of 1788, "from not pre-
ferring the Northern States by a navigation act, it would be politic to increase their
strength by every means in our power; for we had no other resource in our day
of danger than in the naval force of our Northern friends, nor could we ever expect
to become a great nation till we were powerful on the waters."* But "powerful

on the waters " the South can never be. She has live oak, naval stores, and gallant officers; but her climate and its diseases, the bars at the mouth of nearly all her harbors, the *Teredo*, the want of a merchant marine and of fisheries, and the character of her laboring population, will forever prevent her becoming a great naval power. Without the protection of the Navy of the United States, of which the strength centres at the North, she would hold the ingress and egress of every port on her coast at the mercy, I will not say of the great maritime States of Europe, but of Holland, and Denmark, and Austria, and Spain—of any second or third-rate power, which can keep a few steam frigates at sea.

It must be confessed, however, that there is a sad congruity between the conduct of our seceding fellow-citizens and the motives which they assign for it. They attempt a suicidal separation of themselves from a great naval power, of which they are now an integral part, and they put forward, as the reason for this self-destructive course, the legislative measures which have contributed to the growth of the navy. A judicious policy designed to promote that end has built up the commercial and military marine of the Union to its present commanding stature and power; the South, though unable to contribute any thing to its prosperity but the service of her naval officers, enjoys her full share of the honor which it reflects on the country, and the protection which it extends to our flag, our coasts, and our commerce, but under the influence of a narrow-minded sectional jealousy, she is willing to abdicate the noble position which she now fills among the nations of the earth ; to depend for her very existence on the exigencies of the cotton market, to live upon the tolerance of the navies of Europe, and she assigns as leading causes for this amazing fatuity, that the Northern fisheries have been encouraged by a trifling bounty, and that the Northern commercial marine has the monopoly of the coastwise trade. And the politicians, who, for reasons like these, almost too frivolous to merit the time we have devoted to their examination, are sapping a noble framework of government, and drenching a fair and but for them prosperous country in blood, appeal to the public opinion of mankind for the justice of their cause, and the purity of their motives, and lift their eyes to Heaven for a blessing on their arms!

THE TARIFF.

But the tariff is, with one exception, the alleged monster wrong—for which South Carolina in 1832 drove the Union to the verge of a civil war, and which, next to the slavery question, the South has been taught to regard as the most grievous of the oppressions which she suffers at the hands of the North, and that by which she seeks to win the sympathy of the manufacturing States of Europe. It was so treated in the debate referred to. I am certainly not going so far to abuse your patience, as to enter into a discussion of the constitutionality or expediency of the protective policy, on which I am aware that opinions at the North differ, nor do I deem it necessary to expose the utter fallacy of the monstrous paradox, that duties, enhancing the price of imported articles, are paid, not by the consumer of the merchandise imported, but by the producer of the last article of export given in exchange. It is sufficient to say that for this maxim, (the forty-bale theory so called,) which has grown into an article of faith at the South, not the slightest authority ever has been, to my knowledge, adduced from any political economist of any school. Indeed, it can be shown to be a shallow sophism, inasmuch as the *consumer* must be, directly or indirectly, the *producer* of the equivalents given in exchange for the article he consumes. But without entering into this discussion, I shall make a few remarks to show the great injustice of representing the protective system as being in its origin an oppression, of which the South has to complain on the part of the North.

Every such suggestion is a complete inversion of the truth of history. Some attempts at manufactures by machinery were made at the North before the Revolution, but to an inconsiderable extent. The manufacturing system as a great Northern interest is the child of the restrictive policy of 1807—1812, and of the war. That policy was pursued against the earnest opposition of the North, and to the temporary prostration of their commerce, navigation, and fisheries. Their capital was driven in this way into manufactures, and on the return of peace, the foundations of the protective system were laid in the square yard duty on cotton fabrics, in the support of which Mr. Calhoun, advised that the growth of the manufacture would open a new market for the staple of the South, took the lead. As late as 1821 the Legislature of South Carolina unanimously affirmed the constitutionality of protective duties, though denying their expediency,—and of all the States of the Union Louisiana has derived the greatest benefit from this policy ; in fact, she owes the sugar culture to it, and has for that reason given it her steady support. In all the tariff battles while I was a member of Congress, few votes were surer for the policy than that of Louisiana. If the duty on an article imported is considered as added to its price in our market, (which, however, is far from being invariably the case,) the sugar duty, of late, has amounted to a tax of five millions of dollars annually paid by the consumer, for the benefit of the Louisiana planter.

As to its being an unconstitutional policy, it is perfectly well known that the protection of manufactures was a leading and avowed object for the formation of the Constitution. The second law, passed by Congress after its formation, was a revenue law. Its preamble is as follows: " Whereas it is necessary for the support of Government, for the discharge of the debts of the United States, and the encouragement and protection of manufactures, that duties be laid on goods, wares, and merchandise imported." That act was reported to the House of Representatives by Mr. Madison, who is entitled as much as any one to be called the father of the Constitution. While it was pending before the House, and in the first week of the first session of the first Congress, two memorials were presented praying for protective duties ; and it is a matter of some curiosity to inquire, from what part of the country this first call came for that policy, now put forward as one of the acts of Northern oppression, which justify the South in flying to arms. The first of these petitions was from Baltimore. It implored the new Government to lay a protecting duty on all articles imported from abroad, which can be manufactured at home. The second was from the shipwrights, not of New York, not of Boston, not of Portland, but of Charleston, South Carolina, praying for " such a general regulation of trade and the establishment of such a NAVIGATION ACT, as will relieve the particular distresses of the petitioners. in common with those of their fellow-shipwrights throughout the Union " ! and if South Carolina had always been willing to make common cause with their fellow-citizens throughout the Union, it would not now be rent by civil war.

THE COTTON CULTURE INTRODUCED UNDER PROTECTION.

But the history of the great Southern staple is most curious and instructive. His Majesty " King Cotton," on his throne, does not seem to be aware of the influences which surrounded his cradle. The culture of cotton, on any considerable scale, is well known to be of recent date in America. The household manufacture of cotton was coeval with the settlement of the country. A century before the piano-forte or the harp was seen on this continent, the music of the spinning-wheel was heard at every fire-side in town and country. The raw materials were wool, flax, and cotton, the last imported from the West Indies. The colonial system of Great Britain before the Revolution forbade the establishment of any other than household manufactures. Soon after the Revolution, cotton mills were erected in Rhode Island and Massachusetts, and the infant manufacture was encouraged by State duties on the imported fabric. The raw material was still derived exclusively from the West Indies. Its culture in this country was so extremely limited and so little known, that a small parcel sent from the United States to Liverpool in 1784 was seized at the custom-house there, as an illicit importation of British colonial produce. Even as late as 1794, and by persons so intelligent as the negotiators of Jay's treaty, it was not known that cotton was an article of growth and export from the United States. In the twelfth article of that treaty, as laid before the Senate, Cotton was included with Molasses, Sugar, Coffee, and Cocoa, as articles which American vessels should not be permitted to carry from the islands *or from the United States* to any foreign country.

In the Revenue law of 1789, as it passed through the House of Representatives, cotton, with other raw materials, was placed on the free list. When the bill reached the Senate a duty of 3 cents per pound was laid upon cotton, not to encourage, not to protect, but to *create* the domestic culture. On the discussion of this amendment in the House, a member from South Carolina declared that " Cotton was in contemplation " in South Carolina and Georgia, " and *if good seed could be procured he hoped it might succeed.*" On this hope the amendment of the Senate was concurred in, and the duty of three cents per pound was laid on cotton. In 1791, Hamilton, in his report on the manufactures, recommended the repeal of this duty, on the ground that it was " a very serious impediment to the manufacture of cotton," but his recommendation was disregarded.

Thus, in the infancy of the cotton manufacture of the North, at the moment when they were deprived of the protection extended to them before the Constitution by State laws, and while they were struggling against English competition under the rapidly improving machinery of Arkwright, which it was highly penal to export to foreign countries, a heavy burden was laid upon them by this protecting duty, to enable the planters of South Carolina and Georgia to explore the tropics for a variety of cotton seed adapted to their climate. For seven years at least, and probably more, this duty was in every sense of the word a protecting duty. There was not a pound of cotton spun, no not for candle-wicks to light the humble industry of the cottages of the North, which did not pay this tribute to the Southern planter. The growth of the native article, as we have seen, had not in 1794 reached a point to be known to Chief Justice Jay as one of actual or probable export. As late as 1796, the manufacturers of Brandywine in Delaware petitioned

Congress for the repeal of this duty on imported cotton, and the petition was rejected on the Report of a Committee, consisting of a majority from the Southern
States, on the ground, that " to repeal the duty on raw cotton imported would be
to damp the growth of cotton in our own country." Radicle and plumule, root and
stalk, blossom and boll, the culture of the cotton plant in the United States was
in its infancy the foster-child of the Protective System.

When therefore the pedigree of King Cotton is traced, he is found to be the
lineal child of the tariff; called into being by a specific duty ; reared by a tax laid
upon the manufacturing industry of the North, to create the culture of the raw
material in the South. The Northern manufacturers of America were slightly protected in 1789 because they were too feeble to stand alone. Reared into magnitude under the restrictive system and the war of 1812, they were upheld in 1816
because they were too important to be sacrificed, and because the great staple of
the South had a joint interest in their prosperity. King Cotton alone, not in his
manhood, not in his adolescence, not in his infancy, but in his very embryo state,
was pensioned upon the Treasury,—before the seed from which he sprung was
cast " in the lowest parts of the earth." In the book of the tariff " his members were
written, which in continuance were fashioned, when as yet there were none of
them."

But it was not enough to create the culture of cotton at the South, by taxing the
manufactures of the North with a duty on the raw material ; the extension of that
culture and the prosperity which it has conferred upon the South are due to the
mechanical genius of the North. What says Mr. Justice Johnson of the Supreme
Court of the United States, and a citizen of South Carolina? " With regard to the
utility of this discovery " (the cotton gin of Whitney) " the court would deem it a
waste of time to dwell long upon this topic. Is there a man who hears us that has
not experienced its utility ? The whole interior of the Southern States was lan-
guishing, and its inhabitants emigrating, for want of some object to engage their
attention and employ their industry, when the invention of this machine at once
opened views to them which set the whole country in active motion. From child
hood to age it has presented us a lucrative employment. Individuals who were
depressed in poverty and sunk in idleness, have suddenly risen to wealth and
respectability. Our debts have been paid off, our capitals increased, and our lands
trebled in value. We cannot express the weight of obligation which the country
owes to this invention ; the extent of it cannot now be seen."—Yes, and when hap-
pier days shall return, and the South, awakening from her suicidal delusion, shall
remember who it was that sowed her sunny fields with the seeds of those golden
crops with which she thinks to rule the world, she will cast a veil of oblivion over
the memory of the ambitious men who have goaded her to her present madness,
and will rear a monument of her gratitude in the beautiful City of Elms, over the
ashes of her greatest benefactor—ELI WHITNEY.

INTERFERENCE WITH SLAVERY THE GREAT ALLEGED GRIEVANCE.

But the great complaint of the South, and that which is admitted to be the immediate occasion of the present revolt, is the alleged interference of the North in
the Southern institution of slavery ; a subject on which the sensibilities of the two
sections have been so deeply and fearfully stirred, that it is nearly impossible to

speak words of impartial truth. As I have already stated, the declaration of South Carolina, of the causes which prompted her to secede from the Union, alleged no other reason for this movement than the enactment of laws to obstruct the surrender of fugitive slaves. The declaration does not state that South Carolina ever lost a slave by the operation of these laws, and it is doubtful whether a dozen from all the States have been lost from this cause. A gross error on this subject pervades the popular mind at the South. Some hundred of slaves in the aggregate escape annually ; some to the recesses of the Dismal Swamp ; some to the everglades of Florida ; some to the trackless mountain region, which traverses the South ; some to the Mexican States and the Indian tribes ; some across the free States to Canada. The popular feeling of the South ascribes the entire loss to the laws of the free States, while it is doubtful whether these laws cause any portion of it. The public sentiment of the North is not such, of course, as to dispose the community to obstruct the escape or aid in the surrender of slaves. Neither is it at the South. No one, I am told, at the South, not called upon by official duty, joins in the hue and cry after a fugitive ; and whenever he escapes from any States south of the border tier, it is evident that his flight must have been aided in a community of slave-holders. If the North Carolina fugitive escapes through Virginia, or the Tennessee fugitive escapes through Kentucky, why are Pennsylvania and Ohio alone blamed ? On this whole subject the grossest injustice is done to the North. She is expected to be more tolerant of slavery than the South herself ; for while the South demands of the North entire acquiescence in the extremest doctrines of slave property, it is a well-known fact, and as such alluded to by Mr. Clay in his speech on the compromises of 1850, that any man who habitually traffics in this property is held in the same infamy at Richmond and New Orleans that he would be at Philadelphia or Cincinnati.*

While South Carolina, assigning the cause of secession, confines herself to the State laws for obstructing the surrender of fugitives, in other quarters, by the press, in the manifestoes and debates on the subject of secession, and in the official papers of the new Confederacy, the general conduct of the North, with respect to Slavery, is put forward as the justifying, nay, the compelling cause of the revolution. This subject, still more than that of the tariff, is too trite for discussion, with the hope of saying any thing new on the general question. I will but submit a few considerations to show the great injustice which is done to the North, by representing her as the aggressor in this sectional warfare.

The Southern theory assumes that, at the time of the adoption of the Constitution, the same antagonism prevailed as now between the North and South, on the general subject of Slavery ; that, although it existed to some extent in all the States but one of the Union, it was a feeble and declining interest at the North, and mainly seated at the South ; that the soil and climate of the North were soon found to be unpropitious to slave labor, while the reverse was the case at the South ; that the Northern States, in consequence, having, from interested motives, abolished Slavery, sold their slaves to the South, and that then, although the existence of Slavery was recognized, and its protection guaranteed by the Constitution, as soon as the Northern States had acquired a controlling voice in Congress, a persistent and organized system of hostile measures, against the rights of the owners

* See Appendix, C.

of slaves in the Southern States, was inaugurated and gradually extended, in violation of the compromises of the Constitution, as well as of the honor and good faith tacitly pledged to the South, by the manner in which the North disposed of her slaves.

Such, in substance, is the statement of Mr. Davis in his late message ; and he then proceeds, seemingly as if rehearsing the acts of this Northern majority in Congress, to refer to the anti-slavery measures of the State Legislatures, to the resolutions of abolition societies, to the passionate appeals of the party press, and to the acts of lawless individuals, during the progress of this unhappy agitation.

THE SOUTH FORMERLY OPPOSED TO SLAVERY.

Now, this entire view of the subject, with whatever boldness it is affirmed, and with whatever persistency it is repeated, is destitute of foundation. It is demonstrably at war with the truth of history, and is contradicted by facts known to those now on the stage, or which are matters of recent record. At the time of the adoption of the Constitution, and long afterwards, there was, generally speaking, no sectional difference of opinion between North and South, on the subject of Slavery. It was in both parts of the country regarded, in the established formula of the day, as "a social, political, and moral evil." The general feeling in favor of universal liberty and the rights of man, wrought into fervor in the progress of the Revolution, naturally strengthened the anti-slavery sentiment throughout the Union. *It is the South which has since changed, not the North.* The theory of a change in the Northern mind, growing out of a discovery made *soon after* 1789, that our soil and climate were unpropitious to Slavery, (as if the soil and climate then were different from what they had always been,) and a consequent sale to the South of the slaves of the North, is purely mythical—as groundless in fact as it is absurd in statement. I have often asked for the evidence of this last allegation, and I have never found an individual who attempted even to prove it. But however this may be, the South at that time regarded Slavery as an evil, though a necessary one, and habitually spoke of it in that light. Its continued existence was supposed to depend on keeping up the African slave trade ; and South as well as North, Virginia as well as Massachusetts, passed laws to prohibit that traffic ; they were, however, before the revolution, vetoed by the Royal Governors. One of the first acts of the Continental Congress, unanimously subscribed by its members, was an agreement neither to import, nor purchase any slave imported, after the first of December, 1774. In the Declaration of Independence, as originally drafted by Mr. Jefferson, both Slavery and the slave trade were denounced in the most uncompromising language. In 1777 the traffic was forbidden in Virginia, by State law, no longer subject to the veto of Royal Governors. In 1784, an ordinance was reported by Mr. Jefferson to the old Congress, providing that after 1800 there should be no Slavery in any Territory, ceded or to be ceded to the United States. The ordinance failed at that time to be enacted, but the same prohibition formed a part by general consent of the ordinance of 1787, for the organization of the northwestern Territory. In his Notes on Virginia, published in that year, Mr. Jefferson depicted the evils of Slavery in terms of fearful import. In the same year the Constitution was framed. It recognized the existence of Slavery, but the word was carefully excluded from the instrument, and Congress was authorized to abolish the traffic in twenty years. In 1796, Mr. St. George Tucker, law professor in William and Mary College in Virginia, published a treatise entitled, "a Dissertation on Slavery, with a proposal for the gradual abolition of it in the State of Virginia." In the preface to the essay, he speaks of the "abolition of Slavery in this State as an object of the first importance, not only to our moral character and domestic peace, but even to our political salvation." In 1797 Mr. Pinkney, in the Legislature of Maryland, maintained that "by the eternal principles of justice, no man in the State has the right to hold his slave a single hour." In 1803, Mr. John Randolph, from a committee on the subject, reported that the prohibition of Slavery by the ordinance of 1787, was "a measure wisely calculated to promote the happiness and prosperity of the North-western States, and to give strength and security to that extensive frontier." Under Mr. Jefferson, the importation of slaves into the Territories of Mississippi and Louisiana was prohibited in advance of the time limited by the Constitution for the interdiction of the slave trade. When the Missouri restriction was enacted, all the members of Mr. Monroe's Cabinet—Mr. Crawford of Georgia, Mr. Calhoun of South Carolina, and Mr. Wirt of Virginia—concurred with Mr. Monroe in affirming its constitutionality. In 1832, after the Southampton massacre, the evils of Slavery were exposed in the Legislature of Virginia, and the expediency of its gradual abolition maintained, in terms as decided as were ever employed by the most uncompromising agitator. A bill for that object was introduced into the Assembly by the grandson of Mr. Jefferson, and warmly supported by distinguished politicians now on the stage. Nay, we have the recent admission of the Vice-President of the seceding Confederacy, that what he calls "the errors of the past generation," meaning the anti-slavery sentiments entertained by Southern statesmen, "still clung to many as late as *twenty years* ago."

To this hasty review of Southern opinions and measures, showing their accordance till a late date with Northern sentiment on the subject of Slavery, I might add the testimony of Washington, of Patrick Henry, of George Mason, of Wythe, of Pendleton, of Marshall, of Lowndes, of Poinsett, of Clay, and of nearly every first-class name in the Southern States. Nay, as late as 1849, and after the Union had been shaken by the agitations incident to the acquisition of Mexican territory, the Convention of California, although nearly one-half of its members were from the slaveholding States, *unanimously* adopted a Constitution, by which slavery was prohibited in that State. In fact, it is now triumphantly proclaimed by the chiefs of the revolt, that the ideas prevailing on this subject when the Constitution was adopted were fundamentally wrong; that the new Government of the Confederate States "rests upon exactly the opposite ideas; that its foundations are laid and its corner-stone reposes upon the great truth, that the negro is not equal to the white man; that Slavery—subordination to the superior race—is his natural and normal condition. This our new Government is the first in the history of the world based upon this physical, philosophical, and moral truth." So little foundation is there for the statement, that the North, from the first, has been engaged in a struggle with the South on the subject of Slavery, or has departed in any degree from the spirit with which the Union was entered into, by both parties. The fact is precisely the reverse.

NO ANTI-SLAVERY MEASURES ENACTED BY CONGRESS.

Mr. Davis, in his message to the Confederate States, goes over a long list of measures, which he declares to have been inaugurated, and gradually extended, as soon as the Northern States had reached a sufficient number to give their representatives a controlling voice in Congress. But of all these measures, not one is a matter of Congressional legislation, nor has Congress, with this alleged controlling voice on the part of the North, ever either passed a law hostile to the interests of the South, on the subject of Slavery, nor failed to pass one which the South has claimed as belonging to her rights or needed for her safety. In truth, the North, meaning thereby the anti-slavery North, never has had the control of both Houses of Congress, never of the judiciary, rarely of the Executive, and never exerted there to the prejudice of Southern rights. Every judicial or legislative issue on this question, with the single exception of the final admission of Kansas, that has ever been raised before Congress, has been decided in favor of the South; and yet she allows herself to allege " a persistent and organized system of hostile measures against the rights of the owners of slaves," as the justification of her rebellion.

The hostile measures alluded to are, as I have said, none of them matters of Congressional.legislation. Some of them are purely imaginary as to any injurious effect, others much exaggerated, others unavoidably incident to freedom of speech and the press. You are aware, my friends, that I have always disapproved the agitation of the subject of Slavery for party purposes, or with a view to infringe upon the Constitutional rights of the South. But if the North has given cause of complaint, in this respect, the fault has been equally committed by the South. The subject has been fully as much abused there as here for party purposes; and if the North has ever made it the means of gaining a sectional triumph, she has but done what the South, for the last twenty-five years, has never missed an occasion of doing. With respect to every thing substantial in the complaints of the South against the North, Congress and the States have afforded or tendered all reasonable, all possible satisfaction. She asked for a more stringent fugitive slave law in 1850, and it was enacted. She complained of the Missouri Compromise, although adopted in conformity with all the traditions of the Government, and approved by the most judicious Southern statesmen; and after thirty-four years' acquiescence on the part of the people, Congress repealed it. She wished for a judicial decision of the territorial question in her favor, and the Supreme Court of the United States, in contravention of the whole current of our legislation, so decided it. She insisted on carrying this decision into effect, and three new Territories, at the very last session of Congress, were organized in conformity to it, as Utah and New Mexico had been before it was rendered. She demanded a guarantee against amendments of the Constitution adverse to her interests, and it was given by the requisite majority of the two Houses. She required the repeal of the State laws obstructing the surrender of fugitive slaves, and although she had taken the extreme remedy of revolt into her hands, they were repealed or modified. Nothing satisfied her, because there was an active party in the cotton-growing States, led by ambitious men determined on disunion, who were resolved not to be satisfied. In one instance alone the South has suffered defeat. The North, for the first time since the foundation of the Government, has chosen a President by her unaided electoral vote; and that is the occasion of the present unnatural war. I cannot appropriate to myself any portion of those cheers, for, as you know, I did not contribute, by my vote, to that result; but I did enlist under the Banner of "the Union, the Constitution, and the enforcement of the laws." Under that Banner I mean to stand, and with it, if it is struck down, I am willing to fall. Even for this result the South has no one to blame but herself. Her disunionists would give their votes for no candidate but the one selected by leaders who avowed the purpose of effecting a revolution of the cotton States, and who brought about a schism in the Democratic party directly calculated, probably designed, to produce the event which actually took place, with all its dread consequences.

REPRESENTATION OF THREE-FIFTHS OF THE SLAVES.

I trust I have shown the flagrant injustice of this whole attempt to fasten upon the North the charge of wielding the powers of the Federal Government to the prejudice of the South. But there is one great fact connected with this subject, seldom prominently brought forward, which ought forever to close the lips of the South, in this warfare of sectional reproach. Under the old Confederation, the Congress consisted of but one House, and each State, large and small, had but a single vote, and consequently an equal share in the Government, if Government it could be called, of the Union. This manifest injustice was barely tolerable in a state of war, when the imminence of the public danger tended to produce unanimity of feeling and action. When the country was relieved from the pressure of the war, and discordant interests more and more disclosed themselves, the equality of the States became a positive element of discontent, and contributed its full share to the downfall of that short-lived and ill-compacted frame of Government.

Accordingly, when the Constitution of the United States was formed, the great object and the main difficulty was to reconcile the equality of the States, (which gave to Rhode Island and Delaware equal weight with Virginia and Massachusetts,) with a proportionate representation of the people. Each of these principles was of vital importance; the first being demanded by the small States, as due to their equal independence, and the last being demanded by the large States, in virtue of the fact that the Constitution was the work and the Government of the people, and in conformity with the great law in which the Revolution had its origin, that representation and taxation should go hand in hand.

The problem was solved, in the Federal Convention, by a system of extremely refined arrangements, of which the chief was that there should be two Houses of Congress, that each State should have an equal representation in the Senate, (voting, however, not by States, but *per capita*,) and a number of representatives in the House in proportion to its population. But here a formidable difficulty presented itself, growing out of the anomalous character of the population of the slaveholding States, consisting as it did of a dominant and a subject class, the latter excluded by local law from the enjoyment of all political rights, and regarded simply as property. In this state of things, was it just or equitable that the slaveholding States, in addition to the number of representatives to which their free population entitled them, should have a further share in the government of the country, on account of the slaves held as property by a small portion of the ruling class? While property of every kind in the non-slaveholding States was unrepresented, was it just that this species of property, forming a large proportion of the entire property of the South, should be allowed to swell the representation of the slave-holding States ?

This serious difficulty was finally disposed of, in a manner mutually satisfactory, by providing that Representatives and direct Taxes should be apportioned among the States on the same basis of population, ascertained by adding to the whole number of free persons three-fifths of the slaves. It was expected at this time that the Federal Treasury would be mainly supplied by direct taxation. While, therefore, the rule adopted gave to the South a number of representatives out of proportion to the number of her citizens, she would be restrained from exercising this power to the prejudice of the North, by the fact that any increase of the public burdens would fall in the same increased proportion on herself. For the additional weight which the South gained in the presidential election, by this adjustment, the North received no compensation.

But now mark the practical operation of the compromise. Direct taxation, instead of being the chief resource of the Treasury, has been resorted to but four times since the foundation of the Government, and then for small amounts ; in 1798 two millions of dollars, in 1813 three millions, in 1815 six millions, in 1816 three millions again, in all fourteen millions, the sum total raised by direct taxation in seventy-two years, less than an average of 200,000 dollars a year. What number of representatives, beyond the proportion of their free population, the South has elected in former Congresses I have not computed. In the last Congress she was represented by twenty members, in behalf of her slaves, being nearly one-eleventh part of the entire House. As the increasing ratio of the two classes of population has not greatly varied, it is probable that the South, in virtue of her slaves, has always enjoyed about the same proportionate representation in the House, in excess of that accruing from her free population. As it has rarely happened in our political divisions that important measures have been carried by large majorities, this excess has been quite sufficient to assure the South a majority on all sectional questions. It enabled her to elect her candidate for the Presidency in 1800, and thus effect the great political revolution of that year, and is sufficient of itself to account for that approach to a monopoly of the Government which she has ever enjoyed.

Now, though the consideration for which the North agreed to this arrangement, may be said to have wholly failed, it has nevertheless been quietly acquiesced in. I do not mean that in times of high party excitement it has never been alluded to as a hardship. The Hartford Convention spoke of it as a grievance which ought to be remedied ; but even since our political controversies have turned almost wholly on the subject of slavery, I am not aware that this entire failure of the equivalent, for which the North gave up to the South what has secured to her, in fact, the almost exclusive control of the Government of the country, has been a frequent or a prominent subject of complaint.

So much for the pursuit by the North of measures hostile to the interests of the South ;—so much for the grievances urged by the South as her justification for bringing upon the country the crimes and sufferings of civil war, and aiming at the prostration of a Government admitted by herself to be the most perfect the world has seen, and under which all her own interests have been eminently protected and favored; for to complete the demonstration of the unreasonableness of her complaints, it is necessary only to add, that, by the admission of her leading public men, there never was a time when her "peculiar institution" was so stable and prosperous as at the present moment.*

WHY SHOULD WE NOT RECOGNIZE THE SECEDING STATES?

And now let us rise from these disregarded appeals to the truth of history and the wretched subtilties of the Secession School of Argument, and contemplate the great issue before us, in its solemn practical reality. "Why should we not," it is asked, "admit the claims of the seceding States, acknowledge their independence, and put an end at once to the war?" "Why should we not?" I answer the question by asking another : "Why should we?" What have we to gain, what to hope from the pursuit of that course? Peace? But we were at peace before. Why are we not at peace now? The North has not waged the war, it has been forced upon us in self-defence; and if, while they had the Constitution and the Laws, the Executive, Congress, and the Courts, all controlled by themselves, the South, dissatisfied with legal protections and Constitutional remedies, has grasped the sword, can.North and South hope to live in peace, when the bonds of Union are broken, and amicable means of adjustment are repudiated? Peace is the very last thing which Secession, if recognized, will give us; it will give us nothing but a hollow truce,—time to prepare the means of new outrages. It is in its very nature a perpetual cause of hostility ; an eternal never-cancelled letter of marque and reprisal, an everlasting proclamation of border-war. How can peace exist, when all the causes of dissension shall be indefinitely multiplied ; when unequal revenue laws shall have led to a gigantic system of smuggling; when a general *stampede* of slaves shall take place along the border, with no thought of rendition, and all the thousand causes of mutual irritation shall be called into action, on a frontier of 1,500 miles not marked by natural boundaries and not subject to a common jurisdiction or a mediating power? We did believe in peace, fondly, credulously, believed that, cemented by the mild umpirage of the Federal Union, it might dwell forever beneath the folds of the Star-Spangled Banner, and the sacred shield of a common Nationality. That was the great *arcanum* of policy ; that was the State mystery into which men and angels desired to look : hidden from ages, but revealed to us :—

Which Kings and Prophets waited for,
And sought, but never found :

a family of States independent of each other for local concerns, united under one Government for the management of common interests and the prevention of internal feuds. There was no limit to the possible extension of such a system. It had already comprehended half of North America, and it might, in the course of time, have folded the continent in its peaceful, beneficent embrace. We fondly dreamed that, in the lapse of ages, it would have been extended till half the Western hemisphere had realized the vision of universal, perpetual peace. From that dream we have been rudely startled by the array of ten thousand armed men in Charleston Harbor, and the glare of eleven batteries bursting on the torn sky of the Union, like the comet which, at this very moment, burns " In the Arctic sky, and from his

* See Appendix, D.

horrid hair shakes pestilence and war." These batteries rained their storm of iron hail on one poor siege-worn company, because, in obedience to lawful authority, in the performance of sworn duty, the gallant Anderson resolved to keep *his* oath. That brave and faithful band, by remaining at their post, did not hurt a hair of the head of a Carolinian, bond or free. The United States proposed not to reenforce, but to feed them. But the Confederate leaders would not allow them even the poor boon of being starved into surrender; and because *some* laws had been passed *somewhere*, by which it was alleged that the return of *some* slaves (not one from Carolina) had been or might be obstructed, South Carolina, disclaiming the protection of courts and of Congress, which had never been withheld from her, has inaugurated a ruthless civil war. If, for the frivolous reasons assigned, the seceding States have chosen to plunge into this gulf, while all the peaceful temperaments and constitutional remedies of the Union were within their reach, and offers of further compromise and additional guarantees were daily tendered them, what hope, what possibility of peace can there be, when the Union is broken up, when, in addition to all other sources of deadly quarrel, a general *exodus* of the slave population begins, (as, beyond all question, it will,) and nothing but war remains for the settlement of controversies? The Vice-President of the new Confederacy states that it rests on slavery; but from its very nature it must rest equally on war; eternal war, first between North and South, and then between the smaller fragments into which some of the disintegrated parts may crumble. The work of demons has already begun. Besides the hosts mustered for the capture or destruction of Washington, Eastern Virginia has let loose the dogs of war on the loyal citizens of Western Virginia; they are straining at the leash in Maryland and Kentucky; Tennessee threatens to set a price on the head of her noble Johnson and his friends; a civil war rages in Missouri. Why, in the name of Heaven, has not Western Virginia, separated from Eastern Virginia by mountain ridges, by climate, by the course of her rivers, by the character of her population, and the nature of her industry, why has she not as good a right to stay in the Union which she inherited from her Washington, as Eastern Virginia has to abandon it for the mushroom Confederacy forced upon her from Montgomery? Are no rights sacred but those of rebellion; no oaths binding but those taken by men already foresworn; are liberty of thought, and speech, and action nowhere to be tolerated except on the part of those by whom laws are trampled under foot, arsenals and mints plundered, governments warred against, and where their patriotic defenders are assailed by ferocious and murderous mobs?

SECESSION ESTABLISHES A FOREIGN POWER ON THE CONTINENT.

Then consider the monstrous nature and reach of the pretensions in which we are expected to acquiesce; which are nothing less than that the United States should allow a FOREIGN POWER, by surprise, treachery, and violence, to possess itself of one-half of their territory and all the public property and public establishments contained in it; for if the Southern Confederacy is recognized, it becomes a Foreign Power, established along a curiously dove-tailed frontier of 1,500 miles, commanding some of the most important commercial and military positions and lines of communication for travel and trade; half the sea-coast of the Union; the navigation of our Mediterranean Sea, (the Gulf of Mexico, one-third as large as the Mediterranean of Europe,) and, above all, the great arterial inlet into the heart of the Continent, through which its very life-blood pours its imperial tides. I say we are coolly summoned to surrender all this to a Foreign Power. Would we surrender it to England, to France, to Spain? Not an inch of it; why, then, to the Southern Confederacy? Would any other Government on earth, unless compelled by the direst necessity, make such a surrender? Does not France keep an army of 100,000 men in Algeria to prevent a few wandering tribes of Arabs, a recent conquest, from asserting their independence? Did not England strain her resources to the utmost tension, to prevent the native Kingdoms of Central India (civilized States two thousand years ago, and while painted chieftains ruled the savage clans of ancient Britain) from reëstablishing their sovereignty; and shall we be expected, without a struggle, to abandon a great integral part of the United States to a Foreign Power?

Let it be remembered, too, that in granting to the seceding States, jointly and severally, the right to leave the Union, we concede to them the right of resuming, if they please, their former allegiance to England, France, and Spain. It rests with them, with any one of them, if the right of secession is admitted, again to plant a European Government side by side with that of the United States on the soil of America; and it is by no means the most improbable upshot of this ill-starred rebellion, if allowed to prosper. Is this the Monroe doctrine for which the United States have been contending? The disunion press in Virginia last year openly encouraged the idea of a French Protectorate, and her Legislature has, I believe, sold out the James River canal, the darling enterprise of Washington, to a company in France supposed to enjoy the countenance of the emperor. The seceding patriots of South Carolina were understood by the correspondent of the London "Times," to admit that they would rather be subject to a British prince, than to the Government of the United States. Whether they desire it or not, the moment the seceders lose the protection of the United States, they hold their independence at the mercy of the powerful governments of Europe. If the navy of the North should withdraw its protection, there is not a Southern State on the Atlantic or the Gulf, which might not be recolonized by Europe, in six months after the outbreak of a foreign war.

IMMENSE COST OF THE TERRITORIES CLAIMED BY SECESSION.

Then look at the case for a moment, in reference to the cost of the acquisitions of territory made on this side of the continent within the present century,—Florida, Louisiana, Texas, and the entire coast of Alabama and Mississippi; vast regions acquired from France, Spain, and Mexico, within sixty years. Louisiana cost 15,000,000 dollars, when our population was 5,000,000, representing, of course, a burden of 90,000,000 of dollars at the present day. Florida cost 5,000,000 dollars in 1820, when our population was less than 10,000,000, equal to 15,000,000 dollars at the present day, besides the expenses of General Jackson's war in 1818, and the Florida war of 1840, in which some 80,000,000 of dollars were thrown away, for the purpose of driving out a handful of starving Seminoles from the Everglades. Texas cost $200,000,000 expended in the Mexican war, in addition to the lives of thousands of brave men; besides $10,000,000 paid to her in 1850, for ceding a tract of land which was not hers to New Mexico. A great part of the expense of the military establishment of the United States has been incurred in defending the South-Western frontier. The troops, meanly surprised and betrayed in Texas, were sent there to protect her defenceless border settlements from the tomahawk and scalping-knife. If to all this expenditure we add that of the forts, the navy yards, the court-houses, the custom-houses, and the other public buildings in these regions, 500,000,000 dollars of the public funds, of which at least five-sixths have been levied by indirect taxation from the North and North-West, have been expended in and for the Gulf States in this century. Would England, would France, would any government on the face of the earth surrender, without a death-struggle, such a dear-bought territory?

THE UNITED STATES CANNOT GIVE UP THE CONTROL OF THE OUTLET OF THE MISSISSIPPI.

But of this I make no account; the dollars are spent; let *them* go. But look at the subject for a moment in its relations to the safety, to the prosperity, and the growth of the country. The Missouri and the Mississippi Rivers, with their hundred tributaries, give to the great central basin of our continent its character and destiny. The outlet of this mighty system lies between the States of Tennessee and Missouri, of Mississippi and Arkansas, and through the State of Louisiana. The ancient province so-called, the proudest monument of the mighty monarch whose name it bears, passed from the jurisdiction of France to that of Spain in 1763. Spain coveted it, not that she might fill it with prosperous colonies and rising States, but that it might stretch as a broad waste barrier, infested with warlike tribes, between the Anglo-American power and the silver mines of Mexico. With the independence of the United States, the fear of a still more dangerous neighbor grew upon Spain, and in the insane expectation of checking the progress of the Union westward, she threatened, and at times attempted, to close the mouth of the Mississippi, on the rapidly increasing trade of the West. The bare suggestion of such a policy roused the population upon the banks of the Ohio, then inconsiderable, as one man. Their confidence in Washington scarcely restrained them from rushing to the seizure of New Orleans, when the treaty of San Lorenzo El Real in 1795 stipulated for them a precarious right of navigating the noble river to the sea, with a right of deposit at New Orleans. This subject was for years the turning point of the politics of the West, and it was perfectly well understood, that, sooner or later, she would be content with nothing less than the sovereign control of the mighty stream from its head spring to its outlet in the Gulf; *and that is as true now as it was then.*

So stood affairs at the close of the last century, when the colossal power of the first Napoleon burst upon the world. In the vast recesses of his Titanic ambition, he cherished as a leading object of his policy, to acquire for France a colonial empire which should balance that of England. In pursuit of this policy, he fixed his eye on the ancient regal colony which Louis XIV. had founded in the heart of North America, and he tempted Spain by the paltry bribe of creating a kingdom of Etruria for a Bourbon prince, to give back to France the then boundless waste of the territory of Louisiana. The cession was made by the secret treaty of San Ildefonso of the 1st of October, 1800, (of which one sentence only has ever been published, but that sentence gave away half a continent,) and the youthful conqueror concentrated all the resources of his mighty genius on the accomplishment of the vast project. If successful, it would have established the French power on the mouth and on the right bank of the Mississippi, and would have opposed the most formidable barrier to the expansion of the United States. The peace of Amiens, at this juncture, relieved Napoleon from the pressure of the war with England, and every thing seemed propitious to the success of the great enterprise. The fate of America trembled for a moment in a doubtful balance, and five hundred thousand citizens in that region felt the danger, and sounded the alarm.[*]

But in another moment the aspect of affairs was changed, by a stroke of policy, grand, unexpected, and fruitful of consequences, perhaps without a parallel in history. The short-lived truce of Amiens was about to end, the renewal of war was inevitable. Napoleon saw that before he could take possession of Louisiana it would be wrested from him by England, who commanded the seas, and he determined at once, not merely to deprive her of this magnificent conquest, but to contribute as far as in him lay, to build up a great rival maritime power in the West. The Government of the United States, not less sagacious, seized the golden moment— a moment such as does not happen twice in a thousand years. Mr. Jefferson perceived that, unless acquired by the United States, Louisiana would in a short time belong to France or to England, and with equal wisdom and courage he determined that it should belong to neither. True he held the acquisition to be unconstitutional, but he threw to the winds the resolutions of 1798, which had just brought him into power; he broke the Constitution and he gained an Empire. Mr. Monroe was sent to France to conduct the negotiation, in conjunction with Chancellor Livingston, the resident Minister, contemplating, however, at that time only the acquisition of New Orleans and the adjacent territory.

But they were dealing with a man that did nothing by halves. Napoleon knew, *and we know*—that to give up the mouth of the river was to give up its course. On Easter-Sunday of 1803, he amazed his Council with the announcement, that he had determined to cede the whole of Louisiana to the United States. Not less to the astonishment of the American envoys, they were told by the French negotiators, at the first interview, that their master was prepared to treat with them not merely for the Isle of New Orleans, but for the whole vast province which bore the name of Louisiana; whose boundaries, then unsettled, have since been carried on the North to the British line, on the West to the Pacific Ocean; a territory half as big as Europe, transferred by a stroke of the pen. Fifty-eight years have elapsed since the acquisition was made. The States of Louisiana, Arkansas, Missouri, Iowa, Minnesota, and Kansas, the territories of Nebraska, Dacotah, Jefferson, and part of Colorado, have been established within its limits, on this side of the Rocky Mountains; the State of Oregon and the territory of Washington on their western slope; while a tide of population is steadily pouring into the region, destined in addition to the natural increase, before the close of the century, to double the number of the States and Territories. For the entire region west of the Alleghanies and east of the Rocky Mountains, the Missouri and the Mississippi form the natural outlet to the sea. Without counting the population of the seceding States, there are ten millions of the free citizens of the country, between Pittsburg and Fort Union, who claim the course and the mouth of the Mississippi, as belonging to the United States. It is theirs by a transfer of truly imperial origin and magnitude; theirs by a sixty years' undisputed title; theirs by occupation and settlement; theirs by the Law of Nature and of God. Louisiana, a fragment of this Colonial empire, detached from its main portion and first organized as a State, undertakes to secede from the Union, and thinks by so doing that she will be allowed by the Government and People of the United States to revoke this imperial transfer, to disregard this possession and occupation of sixty years, to repeal this law of nature and of God; and she fondly believes that ten millions of the Free People of the Union will allow her and her seceding brethren to open and shut the portals of this mighty region at their pleasure. They may do so, and the swarming millions which throng the course of these noble streams and their tributaries may consent to exchange the charter which they hold from the God of Heaven, for a bit of parchment signed at Montgomery or Richmond; but if I may repeat the words which I have lately used on another occasion, it will be when the Alleghanies and the Rocky Mountains, which form the eastern and western walls of the imperial valley, shall sink to the level of the sea, and the Mississippi and the Missouri shall flow back to their fountains.

Such, Fellow-citizens, as I contemplate them, are the great issues before the country, nothing less, in a word, than whether the work of our noble Fathers of 'the Revolutionary and Constitutional age shall perish or endure; whether this great experiment in National polity, which binds a family of free Republics in one United Government—the most hopeful plan for combining the homebred blessings of a small State with the stability and power of great empire—shall be treacherously and shamefully stricken down, in the moment of its most successful operation, or whether it shall be bravely, patriotically, triumphantly maintained. We wage no war of conquest and subjugation; we aim at nothing but to protect our loyal fellow-citizens, who, against fearful odds, are fighting the battles of the Union in the disaffected States, and to reëstablish, not for ourselves alone, but for our deluded fellow-citizens, the mild sway of the Constitution and the Laws. The result cannot be doubted. Twenty millions of freemen, forgetting their divisions, are rallying as one man in support of the righteous cause—their willing hearts and their strong hands, their fortunes and their lives, are laid upon the altar of the country. We contend for the great inheritance of constitutional freedom transmitted from our revolutionary fathers. We engage in the struggle forced upon us, with sorrow, as against our misguided brethren, but with high heart and faith, as we war for that Union which our sainted Washington commended to our dearest affections. The sympathy of the civilized world is on our side, and will join us in prayers to Heaven for the success of our arms.

APPENDIX.

APPENDIX A. p. 9.

AFTER the remarks in the foregoing address, p. 9, were written, touching the impossibility, at the present day, of *repealing* the instrument by which in 1788 South Carolina gave her consent and ratification to the Constitution of the United States, I sought the opinion on that point of Mr. George Ticknor Curtis, the learned and accurate historian of the Constitution. It afforded me great pleasure to find, from the following letter, that my view of the subject is sustained by his high authority:

JAMAICA PLAINS,
Saturday Evening, *June 8, 1861.*

MY DEAR SIR: Since I came home, I have looked carefully at the ratification of the Constitution by South Carolina. The formal instrument, sent to Congress, seems to be much more in the nature of a Deed or Grant, than of an *Ordinance*. An ordinance would seem to be an instrument adopted by a public body, for the regulation of a subject that in its nature remains under the regulation of that body;—to operate until otherwise ordered. A Deed, or Grant, on the other hand, operates to pass some things; and unless there be a reservation of some control over the subject-matter by the Grantor, his cession is necessarily irrevocable. I can perceive no reason why these distinctions are not applicable to the cession of political powers by a People, or their duly authorized representatives. The question submitted to the People of South Carolina, by the Congress, was, Whether they would cede the powers of government embraced in an instrument sent to them, and called the Constitution of the United States. In other words, they were asked to make a Grant of those Powers. When, therefore, the duly authorized Delegates of the People of South Carolina executed an instrument under seal, declaring that they, " in the name and behalf" of that people, " assent to and ratify the said Constitution," I can perceive no propriety in calling this Deed an *Ordinance*. If they had adopted an instrument entitled, " An Act [or Ordinance] for the government of the People of South Carolina," and had gone on, in the body of the instrument, to declare that the Powers embraced in the Constitution of the United States should be exercised by the agents therein provided, until otherwise ordered, there would have been something left for a repeal to operate upon. But nothing like this was done, and everybody knows that such a ratification could not have been accepted.

There are those, as you are well aware, who pretend that the most absolute and unrestricted terms of cession, which would carry any other subject entirely out of the grantor, do not so operate when the subject of the grant is political sovereignty. But a political school which maintains that a deed is to be construed in one way when it purports to convey one description of right, such as political sovereignty, and in another way when it purports to convey a right of another kind, such as property, would hold a very weak brief in any tribunal of jurisprudence, if the question could be brought to that arbitrament. The American people have been very much accustomed to treat political grants, made by the sovereign power without reservation, as irrevocable conveyances and executed contracts; and although they hold to the right of revolution, they have not yet found out how a deed, absolute on its face, is to be treated in point of law, as a repealable instrument, because it deals with political rights and duties. If any court in South Carolina were now to have the question come before it, whether the laws of the United States are still binding upon their citizens, I think they would have to put their denial upon the naked doctrine of *revolution;* and that they could not hold that, as matter of law and regular political action, their ratification deed of May 23d, 1788, is "repealed" by their late ordinance. Most truly and respectfully yours,

                                                                GEO. T. CURTIS.
MR. EVERETT.

APPENDIX B, p. 22.

Hon. REVERDY JOHNSON to Mr. EVERETT.

                                                    BALTIMORE, 24th June, 1861.
MY DEAR MR. EVERETT.
   I have your note of the 15th, and cheerfully authorize you to use my name, as you suggest.
   The letter I read in the speech which I made in Frederick, should be conclusive evidence that, at its date, Mr. Calhoun denied the right of secession, as a constitutional right, either express or implied.
   But, in addition to this, I had frequent opportunities of knowing that this was his opinion. It was my good fortune to be a member of the Senate of the United States, whilst he was one of its greatest ornaments, for four years, from 1845, until I became a member of Gen. Taylor's administration, and during two sessions (I think 1846 and 1847) I lived in the same house with him. He did me the honor to give me much of his confidence, and frequently his nullification doctrine was the subject of conversation. Time and time again have I heard him, and with ever increased surprise at his wonderful acuteness, defend it on Constitutional grounds, and distinguish it, *in that respect,* from the doctrine of Secession. This last he never, with me, placed on any other ground than that of revolution. This, he said, was to destroy the Government; and no Constitution, the work of sane men, ever provided *for its own destruction.* The other was to preserve it, was, practically, but to amend it, and in a constitutional mode. As you know, and he was ever told, I never took that view. I could see no more constitutional warrant for this than for the other, which, I repeat, he ever in all our interviews repudiated, as wholly indefensible as a constitutional remedy. His mind, with all its wonderful power, was so ingenious that it often led him into error, and at times to such an extent as to be guilty of the most palpable inconsistencies. His views of the tariff and internal improvement powers of the Government, are instances. His first opinions upon both were decided, and almost ultra. His earliest reputation was won as their advocate, and yet four years before his death he denounced both, with constant zeal and with rare power, and, whilst doing so, boldly asserted his uniform consistency. It is no marvel, therefore, with those who have observed his career and studied his character, to hear it stated now that he was the advocate of constitutional secession.
   It may be so, and perhaps is so; but this in no way supports the doctrine, as far as it is rested on his authority. His first views were well considered and formed, without the influence of extraneous circumstances, of which he seemed to me to be often the victim.

Pure in private life and in motives, ever, as I believe and have always believed, patriotic, he was induced, seemingly without knowing it, in his later life, to surrender to section what was intended for the whole, his great powers of analysis and his extraordinary talent for public service. If such a heresy, therefore, as constitutional secession could rest on any individual name, if any mere human authority could support such an absurd and destructive folly, it cannot be said to rest on that of Mr. Calhoun.

With sincere regard, your friend,

REVERDY JOHNSON.

Hon. EDWARD EVERETT, Boston.

APPENDIX C, p. 31.

The number of fugitive slaves, from all the States, as I learn from Mr. J. C. G. Kennedy, the intelligent superintendent of the census bureau, was, in the year 1850, 1,011, being about one to every 3,165, the entire number of slaves at that time being 3,200,364, a ratio of rather more than $\frac{1}{16}$ of one per cent. This very small ratio was diminished in 1860. By the last census, the whole number of slaves in the United States was 3,949,557, and the number of escaping fugitives was 803, being a trifle over $\frac{1}{50}$ of one per cent. Of these it is probable that much the greater part escaped to the places of refuge in the South, alluded to in the text. At all events, it is well known that escaping slaves, reclaimed in the free States, have in almost every instance been restored.

There is usually some difficulty in reclaiming fugitives of any description, who have escaped to another jurisdiction. In most of the cases of fugitives from justice, which came under my cognizance as United States Minister in London, every conceivable difficulty was thrown in my way, and sometimes with success, by the counsel for the parties whose extradition was demanded under the Webster-Ashburton treaty. The French Ambassador told me, that he had made thirteen unsuccessful attempts to procure the surrender of fugitives from justice, under the extradition treaty between the two governments. The difficulty generally grew out of the difference of the jurisprudence of the two countries, in the definition of crimes, rules of evidence, and mode of procedure.

The number of blacks living in Upper Canada and assumed to be all from the United States, is sometimes stated as high as forty thousand, and is constantly referred to, at the South, as showing the great number of fugitives. But it must be remembered that the manumissions far exceed in number the escaping fugitives. I learn from Mr. Kennedy that while in 1860 the number of fugitives was but 803, that of manumissions was 3,010. As the manumitted slaves are compelled to leave the States where they are set free, and a small portion only emigrate to Liberia, at least nine-tenths of this number are scattered through the northern States and Canada. In the decade from 1850 to 1860, it is estimated that 20,000 slaves were manumitted, of whom three-fourths probably joined their brethren in Canada. This supply alone, with the natural increase on the old stock and the new comers, will account for the entire population of the province.

A very able and instructive discussion of the statistics of this subject will be found in the Boston Courier of the 9th of July. It is there demonstrated that the assertion that the Northern States got rid of their slaves by selling them to the South, is utterly unsupported by the official returns of the census.

APPENDIX D, p. 37.

In his message to the Confederate Congress of the 29th April last, Mr. Jefferson Davis presents a most glowing account of the prosperity of the peculiar institution of the South. He states, indeed, that it was "imperilled" by Northern agitation, but he does not affirm (and the contrary, as far as I have observed, is strenuously maintained at the South) that its progress has been checked or its stability in the slightest degree shaken.

I think I have seen statements by Mr. Senator Hunter of Virginia, that the institution of slavery has been benefited and its interests promoted, since the systematic agitation of the subject began; but I am unable to lay my hand on the speech, in which, if I recollect rightly, this view was taken by the distinguished senator.

I find the following extracts from the speeches of two distinguished southern senators, in "The Union," a spirited paper published at St. Cloud, Minnesota :

It was often said at the North, and admitted by candid statesmen at the South, that anti-slavery agitation strengthened rather than weakened slavery. Here are the admissions of Senator Hammond on this point, in a speech which he delivered in South Carolina, October 24, 1858 :—

"And what then (1833) was the state of opinion in the South? Washington had emancipated his slaves. Jefferson had bitterly denounced the system, and had done all that he could to destroy it. Our Clays, Marshalls, Crawfords, and many other prominent Southern men, led off in the colonization scheme. The inevitable effect in the South was that she believed slavery to be an evil—weakness—disgraceful—nay, a sin. She shrunk from the discussion of it. She cowered under every threat. She attempted to apologize, to excuse herself under the plea—which was true—that England had forced it upon her; and in fear and trembling she awaited a doom that she deemed inevitable. But a few bold spirits took the question up—they compelled the South to investigate it anew and thoroughly, and what is the result? Why, it would be difficult to find now a Southern man who feels the system to be the lightest burden on his conscience; who does not, in fact, regard it as an equal advantage to the master and the slave, elevating both, as wealth, strength, and power, and as one of the main pillars and controlling influences of modern civilization, and who is not now prepared to maintain it at every hazard. *Such have been the happy results of this abolition discussion.* "So far *our gain has been immense* from this contest, savage and malignant as it has been."

And again he says :—

"The rock of Gibraltar does not stand so firm on its basis as our slave system. For a quarter of a century it has borne the brunt of a hurricane as fierce and pitiless as ever raged. At the North, and in Europe, they cried 'havoc,' and let loose upon us all the dogs of war. And how stands it now? Why, in this very quarter of a century our slaves have doubled in numbers, and each slave has more than doubled in value. The very negro who, as a prime laborer, would have brought $400 in 1828, would now, with thirty more years upon him, sell for $800."

Equally strong admissions were made by A. H. Stephens, now Vice-President of the "Confederacy," in that carefully prepared speech which he delivered in Georgia in July, 1859, on the occasion of retiring from public life. He then said :—

"Nor am I of the number of those who believe that we have sustained any injury by these agitations. It is true, we were not responsible for them. We were not the aggressors. We acted on the defensive. We repelled assault, calumny, and aspersion, by argument, by reason, and truth. But so far from the institution of African slavery in our section being weakened or rendered less secure by the discussion, *my deliberate judgment is that it has been greatly strengthened and fortified*—strengthened and fortified not only in the opinions, convictions, and consciences of men, but by the action of the Government."